Dear Katerina:

I thank Ch[...] [...]
considering [...] [...]
His service [...] to
the ends of the earth. I wanted to send
this book as a small way to say thank you
but also to share it with you as it blessed me.
I believe the Lord is asking us to seek His
face for revival in the Church and Awakening
in our nation. May our prayers go up before Him.

Realities of
REVIVAL

I pray the grace of our Lord Jesus Christ,
the intense love of God and the intimate
fellowship of the Holy Spirit be multiplied
to you, in you and through you to the
praise of His glory. Thank you,

Your brother,

Justin

Realities of REVIVAL

E . A. JOHNSTON

GOSPEL FOLIO PRESS
www.gospelfolio.com

Published by
GOSPEL FOLIO PRESS
304 Killaly St. West
Port Colborne, ON L3K 6A6, Canada

ISBN 1-897117-19-1

Cover design by Rachel Brooks & Jason Bechtel.

All Scripture quotations from the King James Version
unless otherwise noted.

Ordering Information:
GOSPEL FOLIO PRESS
1-800-952-2382
orders@gospelfolio.com
www.gospelfolio.com

Printed in the United States of America

Contents

Foreword

I commend this fresh look at revival in the twenty-first century by my good friend and colleague, Ernest A. Johnston. Here is a godly layman who spends most of his spare time reading the literary giants on this subject, and then turns the information and inspiration into passionate prayer for God's reviving work in our time.

The short, but succinct, chapters of this book, *The Realities of Revival*, are thought-provoking, heart-searching, and will-bending expressions of his own soul-stirrings. His "view from the pew" is a challenge to pastors and fellow laymen alike. Don't put the book down until you have read the last page!

The sovereign work of God and the responsibility of man in revival are beautifully balanced and blended. Reading the book through for myself, I was forcefully reminded of an expository sermon on revival I heard from the lips of the great Dr. G. Campbell Morgan during my theological studies in London, England—many years ago! What the doctor had to say has helped me to understand how God and man come together in this holy business of praying down revival from heaven.

Let me paraphrase what I heard and remember. Revival is a sovereign work of God. Jesus declared: *"The wind blows where it wishes, and you hear the sound of it, but cannot tell where it comes from and where it goes. So is everyone who is born (or revived) of the Spirit"* (John 3:8).

Only God can command the revival wind. But, we must set our sails to catch that wind when GOD BLOWS! There you have it: we cannot produce revival, but we can ready ourselves to receive it when it comes.

Ernest Johnston shows us in this book how to set our sails. It takes all we have and all that we can do, and God is always faithful to fulfill His promise to breathe on us from the *"four winds" (read Ezek. 37:1-14).*

My lifetime prayer has been for "revival in our time". I have witnessed many such localized movings of God's Spirit, but oh, for a church-wide invasion from heaven! I say again—read this book and join the "revival remnant" until God is pleased to visit us yet again!

Dr. Stephen F. Olford
Founder and Senior Lecturer
The Stephen F. Olford Center for Biblical Preaching
Memphis, Tennessee

Dedication

With warm esteem the following chapters
are dedicated to the memory of

Dr. Stephen F. Olford

his anointed preaching touched thousands,
his holy life modeled Jesus well.

*Give me one hundred men who fear nothing
but God, and hate nothing but sin, and I will
shake the gates of hell.*

—John Wesley

*We have refused the Stone elect and
precious, we have built upon sand of our
own gathering; behold, our houses have
fallen down from the roof to the basement,
and they lie in ruins about our feet, for we
have played the fool before God, and have
not consulted the spirit of wisdom. We have
trusted to ourselves, we have perished in
self-confidence.*

—Joseph Parker

*The typical church is jammed with "pew
potatoes" whose only intent is to come to
church, listen to a sermon, and go away,
hoping that this course will help to privately
smuggle their souls to heaven and help
them to have a reasonably comfortable life
on the way. Any resemblance between this
lifestyle and the Christian life pictured in the
New Testament is purely coincidental.*

—Herb Hodges

And they have not cried unto me with their heart.

—Hosea 7:14

Chapter One
CALL TO AWAKE

"Blow ye the trumpet in Zion, and sound an alarm in my holy mountain: let all the inhabitants of the land tremble: for the day of the LORD cometh, for it is nigh at hand" (Joel 2:1).

When the soldiers in the camp sleep, the enemy storms in and overtakes them. The soldiers may sleep for several reasons. They may be overconfident because of their size and stature. They may be drunk with the cloudiness of debauchery. They may be tired from too much activity. They may be tired from too little activity. Regardless of the reason, if the camp is not guarded with watchmen, the enemy will come in with a flood of destruction.

Today in America and England, two nations once known for upholding the banner of Christ, the church sleeps. It is a deep slumber much akin to a stupor. The cries of the world are drowned out by the snoring church. It has put itself to sleep with much activity—activity done in the name of Christ but without the Spirit of Christ. As the church sleeps upon soft cushions enwrapped with silk sheets in uninterrupted slumber, it is dead to the world as it lazily dreams of work accomplished, tasks completed, budgets met, goals achieved, horizons broadened, planning committees planning, new members joining, money counted, new buildings built, and testimonies of success. Never before has there been more cause for alarm than now. Shhhh! Don't wake the baby, for she is content. What happens when a baby is awakened? It cries. It cries tears.

In J. Sidlow Baxter's Bible (which was given to me by his

widow Isa) he made many interesting notations. In this particular Bible (which was given to him and inscribed by Dan and Bennie Zondervan in 1959), in the gospel of Luke, Dr. Baxter made a unique connection. In chapter nineteen, from verses thirty-six to forty-four, he underlines with his pen an observation relating to our topic of revival. The passage is as follows:

> As He went in the procession, they spread their garments on the road, and as He now approached the point of descending the Mount of Olives, the whole throng of disciples began to be so joyful, they sang praise to God with loud acclaim for all the mighty works they had seen, saying, 'Blessed be the King who comes in the name of the Lord! Peace in heaven and glory in the highest!'
>
> Some of the Pharisees in the crowd spoke to Him, 'Teacher, rebuke your disciples!' And He answered them, I tell you, if these kept silence the stones would cry out!
>
> When He came close to the city and viewed it, He wept over it and said, If you only knew personally even today how you might enjoy peace—but that is now hidden from your eyes. For the time is coming to you, when your enemies shall throw up ramparts around you and shall encircle you and besiege you from every direction, and shall level you and your children within you to the ground, and shall not leave you one stone on another; because you did not understand when you were divinely visited (The Berkeley Version, Luke 19:36-44).

J. Sidlow Baxter had a unique way of marking his Bible. He would use a cross pen and connect passages to reveal their meaning by circling a key phrase. Then he would draw a connecting line to the next key phrase to bring out his commentary. In this particular passage what he did leaps from the page of his Bible. He circled the part of the text, *they sang*, from verse 37 then drew a line with his pen to verse 41 and circled the words, *He wept over it.* He then underlined the following: *"If you only knew personally even today how you might enjoy peace—but that is now hidden from your eyes … you did not understand when you were divinely visited" (v. 42, 44).*

In essence, what Dr. Baxter had noted was this remarkable fact: the world goes on its merry way oblivious to spiritual things. Here God Himself was in their midst and they missed Him. Not only that but while they were singing and dancing and shouting praises He was weeping. He wept over it—over the whole sad display of flesh missing the Divine purpose of redemption for humankind. And today while we dance and shout and praise and sing He weeps still. Jesus Christ is weeping over His bride today because His bride has forsaken Him and played the harlot with the world. God had much to say to His prophet Hosea concerning his harlot wife Gomer (who represented His people Israel). In chapter four of Hosea, in verse one, God states, *"there is no truth, nor mercy, nor knowledge of God in the land".* It was God Himself presenting His case, not against the world at the time, but against His people! Think of it—no knowledge of God in the land. How could He say that about the same people who had witnessed His mighty power and manifestation? He goes on to describe their moral and spiritual state, *"My people are destroyed for lack of knowledge: because thou hast rejected knowledge, I will also reject thee, that thou shalt be no priest to me: seeing thou hast forgotten the law of thy God, I will also forget thy children. As they were increased, so they sinned against me: therefore will I change their glory into shame" (Hos. 4:6-7).*

If we recall God's warning to His people back in the book of Deuteronomy, this is a startling statement made by an indignant God. In Deuteronomy He had warned them of backsliding in prosperity. He had stated in chapter eight of that book,

Beware that thou forget not the Lord thy God, in not keeping his commandments, and his judgments, and his statutes, which I command thee this day:

Lest when thou hast eaten and art full, and hast built goodly houses, and dwelt therein; And when thy herds and thy flocks multiply, and thy silver and thy gold is multiplied, and all that thou hast is multiplied; Then thine heart be lifted up, and thou forget the Lord thy God, which brought thee forth out of the land of Egypt, from the house of bondage;

Who led thee through that great and terrible wilderness, wherein were fiery serpents, and scorpions, and drought, where there was no water; who brought thee forth water out of the rock of flint; Who fed thee in the wilderness with manna, which thy fathers knew not, that he might humble thee, and that he might prove thee, to do thee good at thy latter end;

And thou say in thine heart, My power and the might of mine hand hath gotten me this wealth (Deut. 8:11-17).

So going back to Hosea, God states that there was no knowledge of God in the land and as they increased they sinned against Him. Today in America and England (I cite these two nations, however many more could fall into this pitiful category), we have the same situation and environment in our churches and in the hearts of the people. We are increased with goods and material blessings.

Academically we know our Bibles. We feel our success is well deserved from all our hard work. We take pride in our bigger buildings and larger congregations. Yet while we dance and sing and shout—He weeps! Worse, He vomits because we make Him sick. *"So then because thou art lukewarm and neither cold nor hot, I will spue thee out of my mouth" (Rev. 3:16).* In further describing the lamentable state of the Laodicean church He states, *"Because thou sayest, I am rich, and increased with goods, and have need of nothing; and knowest not that thou art wretched, and miserable, and poor, and blind, and naked" (v. 17).*

Today we know the Word of God better than those before us. We are rich in our knowledge of doctrine. We have more lettered men preaching today than ever before. Yet we have no knowledge of God. We know the book of God but not the God of the book. The majority of our time is spent in study rather than prayer, in planning rather than travailing, in boasting rather than weeping. We do not have a clue about what it is like to be holy. When the world looks at us they see little difference between them and us. And therefore they do not take us seriously or the God we serve, because we do not take seriously the God we claim to serve seriously. The world is in danger as it lies in darkness; it is a powder keg ready to explode. The Church is in greater danger; she is deep in slumber; she must hear and heed the call of God—to awake! Hosea has much to teach us as we move forward.

What I give to Him he takes,
What He takes He cleanses,
What He cleanses He fills,
What He fills He uses.
                    —*J. Sidlow Baxter*

The Word of God cannot be mastered until
we are mastered by the Word of God.
                    —*Stephen F. Olford*

Went into the meetinghouse, ashamed to
see any come to hear such an unspeakable
worthless wretch. However, God enabled
me to speak with clearness, power, and
pungency.
                    —*David Brainerd*

Everyone seems to be holding revival, it's
about time someone let loose of one.
                    —*Vance Havner*

Chapter Two

MORE THAN BURNT OFFERINGS

"For I desired mercy, and not sacrifice; and the knowledge of God more than burnt offerings" (Hos. 6:6).

Israel's heart had become divided. They had begun to trust in the nations around them rather than to trust in God alone. God called them *"a deceitful bow" (Hos. 7:16). "Israel is an empty vine" (v. 10:1).* As Gomer's heart was divided against her husband Hosea (she returned to her harlotry), so Israel had returned to self-reliance and idolatry with the world. God said they had forgotten Him. *"For Israel hath forgotten his Maker, and buildeth temples; and Judah hath multiplied fenced cities: but I will send a fire upon his cities, and it shall devour the palaces thereof" (Hos. 8:14).* The persistent rebellion of Israel. The idolatry of Israel. The multiplied sins of Israel. Eventually God turned them over to their enemies by completely overthrowing them and leading them into captivity in Babylon and Assyria.

What is the application to ourselves in today's age where the shadow of Jesus' return is upon the horizon? There are lessons to be learned here, and one can apply Old Testament prophecy concerning Israel to the Church of today; indeed, these truths from Scripture and the heart of God can be principled to us personally and to the church both locally and universally.

Self examination in light of revealed truth is not only necessary today but mandatory. For we too, like Israel, have strayed away from our Maker. We too are *"an empty vine"* and a *"deceitful bow"*. The activity we produce in the name of Christ, but in the fleshly power of fallible man, is an empty vine. We too are a deceitful bow. This means that the bow and arrow in the hands of the archer cannot be relied upon. Unlike Jonathan's bow, which was reliable, (2 Sam. 1:22) Israel, as an instrument in the hands of God to influence the nations for good and to remain a separate people holy to Him, had become unreliable, and the result of their unreliability was like an empty vine. In short, they had become totally useless to God, and all He could do at that juncture was to chastize them by sending them into captivity until their hearts would return to Him. As Hosea kept taking the unfaithful Gomer back into his house again and again despite her continued whoredom, so God in His forebearance kept reaching down to His people with mercy and extended patience. But the time had come when His patience had turned to wrath and judgement.

Today, in our churches, and especially within our own idolatrous hearts, have we not followed backslidden Israel into the identical critical and lamentable position? As our material successes have enlarged our ministries, we have come to the exact place of self-reliance and idolatry with the world. Pastor, don't kid yourself, be honest. Look at your ministry; who are you relying upon? Your wealthy church member with his big bank account? Your well-earned reputation? Your education? Your own fleshly abilities? Let's face it brethren, we have let the world into the Church and the Church has become sick with "affluencza". We don't look to God any more than Israel did — and see where it got them! Enemies within Arab nations are encircling us as well. And unless we repent crying out to God to forgive us, and confess our sins — the same thing will happen to us. Judgement from an angry God! Don't talk about that — about God being a Judge; why that is not politically correct! A Holy God will judge an evil people. A Holy God will also judge His straying people who are called by His name. In America, and in the Church world-wide today, we are ripe for judgement. Unless we follow the advice laid out in Scripture for revival, we will have judgement. God calls for "more than burnt offerings".

The Apostle Peter warns us that *the time has come for judgment to begin at the house of God"* (1 Pet. 4:17).

The man who is to thunder in the court of Pharaoh with an imperious 'Thus saith the Lord' must first stand barefooted before the burning bush.

—Donald Grey Barnhouse

If a believer fails in prayer, he in fact fails in everything.

—Watchman Nee

For forty years on the lonely slopes of Midian the fiery Moses is schooled. There were graves, if I may so speak, scattered all over the mountainside where hope after hope was buried until at last self went down in utter annihilation.

—F. J. Huegel

Take time to be holy. Speak oft with the Lord.

—W. D. Longstaff

Chapter Three

TIME TO SEEK THE LORD

"Sow to yourselves in righteousness, reap in mercy; break up your fallow ground: for it is time to seek the Lord, till he come and rain righteousness upon you" (Hos. 10:12).

God in His mercy has given, to His straying people, instruction for revival in his Word. How few have taken this instruction over the centuries! Those who have (Charles Finney to name one) have proven God and His word to be reliable and true. God is the Father in the parable of the prodigal son. As we go about on our wilful and self-destructive way, He watches us from afar. We are never out of His sight. He is waiting for our return. And He will welcome us with open arms, placing a ring upon our finger to show family relationship once again. When will we, like the prodigal, realize our pitiful condition? When we look in the mirror and see ourselves as God sees us rather than how man sees us. Brethren, it is time to lay aside the church planting books. Lay aside our plans, our agendas. It is time to rely upon Him and His wisdom. Still we rely upon ourselves and stay busy, busy, busy in much activity. Alas, the Church has sadly strayed from her Bridegroom. God today feels like Hosea did about Gomer back then—we are breaking His heart.

God desires obedience from us, not programs. He will not honor a church "planted" in the flesh. He will not honor a lack of reverence in His house of prayer. He will not honor the watering down of His holy Word to appeal to a larger mass of people. He will not honor the acceptance of His Son to be based on a formula and an intellectual agreement to a few questions pertaining to His gospel. So what do we do? How can we escape this dreaded disease of modern church activity that has shut out completely the Third Person of the Godhead—the Holy Spirit? Let us follow the Book.

When a Christian strays from the purpose of God, the problem is not in any thing but in the heart. In the Old Testament, when individuals failed, it was a problem of the heart. King Saul let his pride rule him rather than his heart and he ended his life by saying, *"I have played the fool, and have erred exceedingly" (1 Sam. 26:21)*. King David let his lust rule him in the case of Bathsheba and then his pride covered the sin for nearly two years—all because of the hardening of his heart. It took the parable of Nathan about the poor man's lamb to break up the fallow ground of his hard heart. One can observe the true revival of his heart and repentance over his sins in Psalm fifty-one.

To better understand this issue of the heart *("Keep thy heart with all diligence; for out of it are the issues of life" (Prov. 4:23))* regarding the illustration of fallow ground and revival, let us turn to one of the experts on the subject. I defer to the wisdom of Charles Grandison Finney. His *LECTURES ON REVIVAL* is a classic on the subject. In his chapter "How to Promote a Revival", he discusses clearly what Hosea stated centuries earlier. Some students of revival claim adamantly that revival cannot be promoted; it is solely a sovereign work of God. I disagree. Jonathan Goforth had revival in China using Finney's scriptural methods. And so have others. Brethren, rather than disagreeing with what brings revival, let us pray and repent and follow the Scripture—then let God reveal Himself in His sovereignty. Finney brilliantly writes:

> The Jews were a nation of farmers. Scripture therefore commonly draws illustrations from

that line of work, and from scenes farmers and shepherds would know well. So when the prophet Hosea addresses Israel as a nation of backsliders, reproving their idolatry and threatening them with the judgements of God, he uses fallow ground as his illustration. Fallow ground is ground once farmed but which now lies waste. It must be broken up again before it is ready to be planted.... . Now a revival consists of two parts: revival within the church and revival among the ungodly.

What does it mean to "break up the fallow ground"? To break up the fallow ground is to break up your hearts—to prepare your minds to bring forth fruit to God. The Bible often compares the human mind to ground, and the Word of God to seed sown in it. The fruit represents the actions and desires of those who receive it. To break up the fallow ground, then, is to bring the mind into a state where it is fitted to receive the Word of God. Sometimes your heart becomes matted down, hard and dry and fallen to waste. It will bear no fruit until it is broken up, readied to receive the Word of God. It is this softening of the heart, making it feel the truth, which the prophet calls "breaking up your fallow ground."

Finney then goes on to describe how one goes about breaking up the fallow ground. It is by self examination. Examining the state of your heart. Asking the Holy Spirit to shed His holy search light upon your sins. Finney lists both sins of omission and sins of commission. It matters little who you are or how big your ministry is, you would be hard pressed not to find yourself listed somewhere in his detailed list of sins such as neglecting prayer, unbelief, lack of care for the lost, pride, and hypocrisy.

This leads us to our next topic:

- What is true revival?
- How we can take our church through the process of praying for revival?
- How we can experience personal revival?

"If there is a room nobody wants, give that to me."
—Samuel Morris, when asked by the
President of Taylor University
what dorm room he wanted.

God doesn't tell a person first by his head; He
tells him first by the heart. God put it in my
heart and made me long to go to China.
—C. T. Studd

We Christians ought to be the cleanest,
purest, most righteous, holiest people in all
the world.
—A. W. Tozer

When we were born again, we were born at
the Cross, born crucified.
—L. E. Maxwell

Chapter Four

WHAT IS TRUE REVIVAL?

"Will you not revive us again; that your people may rejoice in you?" (Ps. 85:6).

Let us begin with the common misconception of revival. Revival is not having a tent meeting, serving hot dogs, and enlisting a traveling evangelist to come in and preach and hope for some converts. Nor is it taking your church through a "program" or "topic of the year" and hoping some people will be converted and more members will serve in the nursery. No, no, no. A true revival is a visitation of God. It is when the glory of the divine presence descends upon the people. It is an awakening of a sleeping church, and it manifests itself in the church by its members becoming totally broken and yielded to Jesus Christ as Lord. Inwardly, Christians become Christ-like in nature and in behavior. Accompanying this is such a dramatic change in life-patterns that the ungodly are awakened and come into the kingdom usually with deep conviction of sin and repentance toward God.

Such was the case in England, when George Whitefield preached and God revived that country from a deep spiritual slumber. In the mid 1700's, God visited His people through the remarkable field preaching of George Whitefield. We have an account, "The open firmament above me, the prospect of the adjacent fields, with the sight of thousands and thousands, some in coaches, some on horseback, and some in the trees, and at times all affected and drenched in tears together".

During this eighteenth-century revival, John Wesley was

used of God as well. John Wesley commented on the strange phenomenon of people crying out and falling down with the conviction of their sins upon them. "My voice could scarce be heard amidst the groanings of some and the cries of others... . A Quaker who stood by ... was biting his lip and knitting his brows, when he dropped down as thunder-struck. The agony he was in was even terrible to behold."

Around this time what has come to be known as "THE GREAT AWAKENING" occurred in America under the ministry of Jonathan Edwards. In New England in Northampton, Jonathan Edwards preached his famous sermon, "Sinners In The Hand of An Angry God", during which many in the congregation fell down as dead, crying out in agony and holding onto the pillars in the church so as not to slip into the depths of hell. George Whitefield joined with Edwards and revival swept the land like a wildfire. To capture a glimpse of the excitement which occurred during this epoch in history I defer to an account of farmer, Nathan Cole, who attended a open air meeting preached by Whitefield at this hour in history in America. The year was 1740 and here is this man's account:

> Now it pleased God to send Mr. Whitefield into this land and my hearing of his preaching at Philadelphia, like one of the old apostles, and many thousands flocking after him to hear the gospel and great numbers converted to Christ, I felt the Spirit of God drawing me by conviction ... Next I heard he was on Long Island and next at Boston and next at Northampton and then, one morning, all of a sudden, about 8 or 9 o'clock there came a messenger and said, "Mr. Whitefield preached at Hartford and Wethersfield yesterday and is to preach at Middletown this morning at 10 o'clock". I was in my field, at work, I dropped my tool that

I had in my hand and ran home and ran through my house and bade my wife get ready quick to go and hear Mr. Whitefield preach at Middletown and ran to my pasture for my horse with all my might, fearing I should be too late to hear him. I brought my horse home and soon mounted and took my wife up and went forward as fast as I thought the horse could bear, and when my horse began to be out of breath I would get down and put my wife in the saddle and bid her ride as fast as she could and not stop or slack for me except I bade her, and so I would run until I was almost out of breath and then mount my horse again, and so I did several times to favour my horse ... for we had twelve miles to ride double in little more than an hour.

On high ground I saw before me a cloud or fog rising, I first thought it was from the great river but as I came nearer the road I heard a noise something like a low rumbling of horses feet coming down the road and this cloud was a cloud of dust made by the running of horses feet. It arose some rods in the air, over the tops of the hills and trees, and when I came within about twenty rods of the road I could see men and horses slipping along in the cloud like shadows and when I came nearer it was like a steady stream of horses and their riders, scarcely a horse more than his length behind another, all of a lather and some with sweat... .

We went down with the stream, I heard no man speak a word all the way, three miles, but everyone pressing forward in great haste, and when we got down to the old meetinghouse there was a great multitude — it was said to be 3000 or 4000 people assembled together. We got off from our horses and shook off the dust, and the ministers were then coming to the meetinghouse. I turned and looked towards the great river and saw ferry boats running swift, forward and backward, bringing over loads of people, the oars rowed nimble and quick. Everything, men, horses and boats, all seemed to be struggling for life, the land and the banks over the river looked black with people and horses. All along the 12 miles I saw no man at work in his field but all seemed to be gone.

God came down and many souls were brought into His kingdom. Next we turn to the work of Charles Finney in upstate New York. Particularly in a village called Antwerp around 1830.

*If Finney is right, I vowed, then I'm going to
find out what those laws are and obey them,
no matter what it costs.*

—Jonathan Goforth

*Let the gospel be preached and the Spirit
poured out, and you will see that it has
such power to change the conscience,
to ameliorate the conduct, to raise the
debased, to chastise and to curb the
wickedness of the race, that you must glory
in it. I say, there is nought like the power of
the Spirit.*

—C. H. Spurgeon

*In those days came John the Baptist,
preaching in the wilderness of Judaea,
And saying, Repent ye: for the kingdom of
heaven is at hand.*

—Matthew 3:1-2

*All the evil you do because you don't have
the Spirit adds to your guilt, you dishonor
Christianity. You trip the church and the world.
And your guilt is enlarged by your influence.
This we will see on Judgement Day.*

—Charles G. Finney

Chapter Five
FINNEY'S FIRE

"For they have sown the wind, and they shall reap the whirlwind"
(Hos. 8:7).

In his memoirs, Charles G. Finney recalled (while in his 70's) the events which preceded and followed the spiritual awakening in the eastern part of America during the 18th century. We will cite one example of his revival work only to show how God revealed Himself to saints and sinners alike in a unique manifestation of grace and conversion during this period in Christian history. Whatever one's feelings about Finney (he indeed had peculiar traits and some error in his doctrine, especially on perfection), few can argue with the results of his ministry and the work of the Holy Spirit upon it. In this particular incident, which occurred in New York in the year of 1824, we will see in his own words the manifestation of a Holy God upon a wicked town.

> I must now give some account of my labors and their results, at Antwerp, a village north of Evans' Mills. I arrived there the first time in April, and found that no religious services of any kind were held in that town. ... I very soon learned that there was a Presbyterian church in that place, consisting of but few members. They had some years before tried to keep up a meeting at the village on the Sabbath. But one of the elders who conducted their Sabbath meeting lived about five miles out

of the village, and was obliged, in approaching the village, to pass through a Universalist settlement. The Universalists had broken up their village meeting by rendering it impossible for Deacon Randall, as they called him, to get through their village and get to meeting. They would even take off the wheels of his carriage; and finally they carried their opposition so far that he gave up attending meetings at the village; and all religious services at the village, or in the township so far as I could learn were relinquished altogether.

In passing around the village I heard a vast amount of profanity. I thought I had never heard so much in any place that I had ever visited. It seemed as if the men in playing ball upon the green, and in every business place that I stepped into, were all cursing and swearing, and damning each other. I felt as if I had arrived upon the borders of hell. I had a kind of awful feeling, I recollect, as I passed around the village on Saturday. The very atmosphere seemed to me to be poison; and a kind of terror took possession of me. I gave myself to prayer on Saturday, and finally urged my petition till this answer came: *"Be not afraid to speak, and hold not thy peace; for I am with thee, and no man shall set on thee to hurt thee. For I have much people in this city" (Acts 18:9-10).* This completely relieved me of all fear. I found, however, that the Christian people there were really afraid that something serious might happen if religious meetings were established in that place again.

Through the help of a Christian woman named Mrs. Howe who opened her home to him to have a service, they were able to procure the local school house for a meeting next Sunday. This day arrived, Finney preached and many were influenced by his message. From this service they were able to obtain a village church for his next few preaching engagements. We shall return to his observations:

> On the third Sabbath that I preached there an aged man came to me as I came out of the pulpit, and asked me if I would]go and preach in a school house in his neighborhood, saying that they had never had any services there. He told me that it was about three miles in a certain direction. He wished me to come as soon as I could. I appointed the next day, Monday, at five o'clock in the afternoon. It was a warm day. I left my horse at the village and thought I would walk down, so that I should have no trouble in calling along on the people in the neighborhood of the school house on my way. However before I got to the place, having labored so hard on the Sabbath, I found myself very much exhausted, and sat down by the way and felt as if I could scarcely proceed. I blamed myself for not having taken my horse.
>
> When I arrived at the appointed hour I found the school house full; and I could only get a standing place near the door, which stood open— and the windows were all open. I read a hymn— and I cannot call it singing, for they seemed never to have had any church music in that place. However, they pretended to sing. But it amounted to about this: each one bawled in his own way. My ears had been cultivated by teaching church music; and their horrible discord distressed me so much that at first I thought I must go out. I finally

put both hands over my ears and held them with the full strength of my arms. But this did not shut out the discords. I held my head down over my knees, with my hands on my ears, and shook my head, and tried as far as possible to get rid of the horrible discords that seemed almost to make me mad. I stood it however until they were through; and then I cast myself down on my knees almost in a state of desperation, and began to pray. The Lord opened the windows of heaven and the Spirit of prayer was poured out, and I let my whole heart out in prayer.

I had taken no thought with regard to a text upon which to preach; but waited to see the congregation, as I was in the habit of doing in those days, before I selected a text. As soon as I had done praying, I arose from my knees and said: "Up, get ye out this place; for the Lord will destroy this city". I said I did not recollect where the text was; but I told them very nearly where they would find it, and then went on to explain it. I said that there was such a man as Abraham, and also who he was; and that there was such a man as Lot, and who he was; their relations to each other; their separating from each other on account of differences between their herdmen; and that Abraham took the hill country, and Lot settled in the vale of Sodom. I then told them how exceedingly wicked Sodom became, and what abominable practices they fell into. I told them that the Lord decided to destroy Sodom, and visited Abraham and informed him what He was about to do. That Abraham prayed to the Lord to spare Sodom if He found so many righteous there; and the Lord promised to do so for their sakes. That then Abraham besought Him to save it for certain less number; and the Lord said He would spare it for their sakes. That he kept on reducing the number until he reduced the number of righteous persons to ten; and God promised him that if He found ten righteous persons in the city, He would spare it. Abraham made no further request, and Jehovah left him. But it was found that there was but one righteous person there, and that was Lot, Abraham's nephew. *"And the men said to Lot, Hast thou here any besides? Son-in-law, and thy sons, and thy daughters, and whatsoever thou hast in the city, bring them out of this place; for we will destroy this place, because the cry of them is waxen great before the face of the Lord; and the Lord hath sent us to destroy it. And Lot went out and spake unto his sons-in-law, which married his daughters, and said, Up, get you out of this place, for the Lord will destroy the city. But he seemed as one that mocked unto his sons-in-law"* (Gen. 19:12-14).

While I was relating these facts I observed the people looked as if they were angry. Many of the men were in their shirt sleeves; and they looked at each other and at me, as if they were ready to pitch into me and chastise me for something on the spot. I saw their strange and unaccountable looks, and could not understand what I was saying that had offended them. However, it seemed to me that their anger arose higher and higher as I continued the narrative. As soon as I had finished the narrative I turned upon them and said, that I understood that they had never had a religious meeting in that place; and that therefore I had a right to take it for granted, and was compelled to take it for granted that they were an ungodly people. I pressed that home upon them with more and more energy, with my heart full to bursting.

I had not spoken to them in this strain of direct application, I should think more than a quarter of an hour, when all at once an awful solemnity seemed to settle down upon them; and a some thing flashed over the congregation—a kind of shimmering, as if there was some agitation in the atmosphere itself. The congregation began to fall from their seats; and they fell in every direction, and cried for mercy. If I had had a sword in each hand I could not have cut them off their seats as fast as they fell. Indeed nearly the whole congregation were either on their knees or prostrate, I should think, in less than two minutes from this first shock that fell upon them. Every one prayed for himself, who was able to speak at all. I, of course was obliged to stop preaching, for they no longer paid any attention.

When I went down the second time I got an explanation of the anger manifested by the congregation during the introduction of my first sermon there. I learned that the place was called Sodom—but I knew it not; and that there was one pious man in the place, and him they called Lot. This was the old man that invited me there. The people supposed that I had chosen my subject, and preached to them in that manner, because they were so wicked as to be called Sodom. This was a striking coincidence; but as far as I was concerned, it was altogether accidental.

I have not been in that place for many years. A few years since I was laboring in Syracuse in the State of New York. Two gentlemen called upon me one day; one quite an elderly man, another perhaps a man of 47 years of age. The younger man introduced the older one to me as Deacon White, and elder in his church; saying that he had called on me to give a hundred dollars to Oberlin college. The older man in his turn introduced the younger; saying, "This is my minister, the Rev. Mr. Cross. He was converted under your ministry". Whereupon Brother Cross said to me: Do you remember preaching at such a time in Antwerp, and in such a part of the town in a school house in the afternoon, and that such a scene—describing it—occurred there? I said, "I remember it very well, and can never forget it while I remember anything". "Well", said he, "I was then but a young man, and was converted in that meeting". He has been many years a successful minister.

Some other examples of revival will be presented as well as we proceed.

The best means of keeping near to God is in the closet. Here the battle is won or lost.
                                        —Edward Payson

We see that God is faithful and never will forget the promises that he has made to his church, and that he will not suffer the smoking flax to be quenched, even when the floods seem to be overwhelming it, but will revive the flame again, even in the darkest times.
                                        —Jonathan Edwards

Such a sight I never saw before. I believe there were no less than fifty thousand people, and near four score coaches, besides great number of horses. God gave me great enlargement of heart. I continued my discourse for an hour and a half, and when I returned home, I was filled with such love, peace and joy that I cannot express it.
                                        —George Whitefield

Is there any sin in your past that you have not confessed to God? Is there anything in your life that is doubtful?
                                        —Evan Roberts

Chapter Six

WHEN GOD COMES DOWN TO VISIT MAN

"Who shall ascend into the hill of the Lord? or who shall stand in his holy place? He that hath clean hands, and a pure heart; who hath not lifted up his soul unto vanity, nor sworn deceitfully. He shall receive the blessing from the Lord, and righteousness from the God of his salvation. This is the generation of them that seek him, that seek thy face, O Jacob. Selah" (Ps. 24:3-6).

In this chapter we shall study the great revival of Wales in 1904. Why? Because your average Christian has never heard of it. It is doubtful that your average minister has ever truly studied it much less made an effort to try to align his life to it. God visits His people in a supernatural and sovereign way. He does not follow a church program or a method that is geared around the planning of man to empower the plans of man. He does not care about the strength of your ministry or the largeness of your buildings or the reputation you have built for yourself. He cares only that man will seek him fervently with a contrite heart and then it is His pleasure to reveal Himself to man, to show His glory and majesty and authority, and for man to honor Him and His dear Son.

We will study the revival in the little country of Wales. Isn't the Creator of the universe displaying a sense of irony showing how He works by choosing a tiny hamlet to reveal Himself rather than choosing a great city with teeming crowds and commerce? His ways are not our ways, neither are our

41

thoughts His thoughts. He is not searching for important men and famous places. Rather, the Lord of Hosts looks for men and women whose hearts seek Him with a burning, all consuming passion. The end result of revival is this very thing. Men and women seek Him with a burning all consuming passion. They seek His presence. They desire His holiness. They pray for His Spirit. They tell others about the work of His Son on Calvary's cross. And somewhere in all of this, humankind sees God for who He is and what He is and many souls are saved from the torments of everlasting fire.

Isn't this our mission? It is not to build ball fields or recreation halls to play our little games and exercise our flesh, but rather it is to preach Christ and Him crucified and to live holy lives seeking and honoring God in all we do. We need to revive the prayer meeting in the church. Rather than have it remain what it is—either a fellowship supper or preaching opportunity—let it be what it should: a time for God's people to gather and confess their sins, to cry out to the God of Glory, seeking Him with contrite hearts and a burning passion in thankfulness for saving wretches like we truly are. Oh Lord, rend your heavens! Come visit your poor pitiful people once more. Please Lord, before the end comes and our time is gone.

There was a young man of twenty-six by the name of Evan Roberts. Completely unknown to Christendom at the time, he believed in two things: prayer and the truth of Scripture. Through the prayers of this Elijah of a man, famous men such as G. Campbell Morgan and F. B. Meyer came from London to Wales to stand in the back of rooms with their mouths agape and their heads bowed to witness the glory of God.

We will begin our recount of this moving of God by stating this fact: Evan Roberts was only a figure in the revival; it did not begin with him. It had begun in the hearts of God's people who were led by the Holy Spirit to pray, yet God used this young man to fan the flame of his scorching fire that burned the chaff from the hearts of strong men who were known infidels in that little community. This place in revival history shows how God deals with humankind through the prayers of His saints. Mainly, this is what occurred: a praying minority humbled themselves before a Holy God and sought His Face for the good of humankind and in turn a Holy God invaded a tiny country. He humbled the most wicked sinners in that area with His divine presence. Man did not share in God's glory, and consequently many were saved for eternity. How many? It is recorded that nearly 100,000 conversions occurred in Wales in 1904-1905.

Though it is impossible to capture the true essence of divine work, here are some reports from that period in history:

> GREAT CROWDS OF PEOPLE DRAWN TO LOUGHOR—Congregations stay till half-past-two in the morning. A remarkable religious revival is now taking place at Loughor. For some days a young man named Evan Roberts, a native of Loughor, has been causing great surprise at Moriah Chapel. The place has been beseiged by dense crowds of people unable to obtain admission. Such excitement has prevailed that the road on which the chapel is situated has been lined with people from end to end. Roberts, who speaks in Welsh, opens his discourse by saying that he does not know what he is going to say but that when he is in communion with the Holy Spirit, the Holy Spirit will speak, and he will simply be the medium of His wisdom. The preacher soon after launches out into a fervent and, at times, impassioned oration. His statements have had most stirring effects upon his listeners. Many who have disbelieved Christianity for years are again returning to the

fold of their younger days. One night, so great was the enthusiasm invoked by the young revivalist that, after his sermon which lasted two hours, the vast congregation remained praying and singing until two-thirty in the morning! Shop-keepers are closing early in order to get a place in the chapel, and tin and steel workers throng the place in their working clothes.

HOLYHEAD—In this important town a drunken man is a thing of the past and the police are having an easy time of it. 500 converts have been reported.

RHONDDA VALLEY—A scene which may be witnessed any morning here at 5 a.m. Scores of miners hold a service before going home from the midnight shift. The Superintendent starts a hymn, "In the deep and mighty ocean", and then the pit re-echoes the song. An old man whose grey head is tinged with coal dust falls on his knees to pray. Others do the same. The service attracts men from different workings and flickering lights are seen approaching the improvised temple. "Now, boys, those of you who love Christ, UP WITH YOUR LAMP!" cries a young miner. In a second, scores of lights flicker in the air and another song of thanks sets the mine ringing.

GLYNNEATH—The two independent churches ADDOLDY AND CAPEL-Y-GLYN which had been on unbrotherly terms for a period of nearly twelve years have been reconciled and united meetings have been held. The two ministers shook hands before a united church of nearly 400 members.

MAESTEG—An insurance agent told a reporter that at practically every house he called at after Christmas he was met by the wife with a happy smile and these words, "This is the happiest Christmas we have ever had". Their husbands had been converted and stopped their wastage of money in gambling and drunkenness.

CARNARVON—Details have just reached us of wonderful meetings. The influence of the Holy Spirit is felt most powerfully by men and women alike. Strong men pale and tremble. Young men and women storm the gates of heaven with overwhelming importunity and overpowering effect. The whole congregation is completely melted into pronounced weeping and sobbing. Large numbers are finding the Lord. Two well-known reprobates came forward and sank on their knees and began to beat their breasts.

The Bible Society's records show that over three times the number of Bibles are now being sold since the revival broke out. The book-sellers say it is no trouble now to sell Bibles; the trouble is to get them.

Longstanding debts were paid, stolen goods returned, drinking taverns forsaken, oaths ceased to be heard so that it was said in the mines the horses could not understand the language of their drivers. Political meetings had to be postponed as members of the Houses of Parliament were found taking part in the revival meetings. Theatrical companies made sure that they did not come to Wales as they knew that there they would go bankrupt. Magistrates were presented with white gloves in many places to signify that there were no arrests.

The prisons were empty. Even in the universities, revival scenes were commonplace day after day for months ... over 70,000 names of converts are reported just two months after the lifestreams broke out!

Such were the remarkable scenes in Wales from 1904 through 1905. Crime ceased. Taverns closed. People made their way home in the wee small hours of the morning, holding hands and singing hymns beneath a starlit sky. Even ministers at odds with each other united—when this happens it can only be explained as true revival!

We will continue our study with a manifestation of God in a local church where the author was a witness to the glory of God descending.

God can only bless with the anointing of His Spirit those who pursue a life of holiness.
—Stephen F. Olford

God is in a league offensive and defensive with thee, but he looks to be called.
—William Gurnall

And the Lord turned, and looked upon Peter. And Peter remembered the word of the Lord, how he had said unto him, Before the cock crow, thou shalt deny me thrice. And Peter went out and wept bitterly.
—Luke 22:61-62

I am ashamed to be a member of the church of Jesus Christ today.
—Leonard Ravenhill

Chapter Seven

TEARS BETWEEN
THE PORCH AND THE ALTAR

"Let the priests, the ministers of the Lord, weep between the porch and the altar, and let them say, Spare thy people, O Lord" (Joel 2:17).

There seems to be a pattern in Revival which is undeniable. The pattern is as follows:

- Prayer is the first and foremost thing.
- People begin to confess their personal sins.
- A new reverence for God takes place in a dramatic fashion.
- A sense of the Holy Spirit pervades the atmosphere.
- There is brokenness among the people and much weeping.
- Christians return to their first love of Christ.
- The lost are swept in like an ocean wave. True converts are numerous.
- There is an undescribable presence of God felt by all.

I will attempt to explain a personal encounter with this phenomenon. Sadly, words will not do justice to the event itself. A manifestation of God cannot be explained by mortals. This is merely an attempt to explain how true revival visited in a local church in a small town.

For my part it began in prayer. At the time I was discipling a group of men each week in my home. God placed it on some of our hearts to pray for revival. I had recently led the men through the book by Charles Finney, *LECTURES ON REVIVAL.*

A few of us began to meet between 6 a.m. and 7:30 a.m. each Monday and Thursday in the chapel of our church. This was in 1993 and 1994. We sought the Lord in tears and travail asking for revival to come and to be a witness to it. We were praying for it to come to our church. It did not come to our church but to a church in a distant town—God in His faithfulness allowed us to witness this mighty moving of His Spirit.

I will preface my remarks with the fact that local revival (where the moving of the Holy Spirit is centered in a specific locality) and church revival (where the moving of the Holy Spirit is centered upon a particular local church) is widespread and common to church history. Some cases have been documented by the local township, university, church, and so forth, others have not. This particular revival which the author was witness to has not heretofore been documented in a published format. It is only one of many movements of God in history which occur at the hand of His sovereignty in the places of His choosing. If I may make a bold statement, which can be supported by Scripture, God is searching His planet Earth for men and women who cry out to Him through tears over sin in the world and seek a manifestation of His power to reveal His glory to humankind, with the end result of lost individuals being brought into His kingdom for eternity and to complete the body of Christ, the Church, which will, as the Bride, be presented to the Bridegroom on that glorious day.

A man whom I was discipling and I were led by the Spirit of God to visit a church in a little town in the state of Mississippi which before had been unknown to us. As I have mentioned, we had been praying for revival for a period of time on a regular basis. God answered our travailing prayers by allowing us to partake in the visitation of His Spirt. This is the record of that evening in 1994:

It was on a hot, humid, Saturday evening that we ventured to a little church where we had heard that God was sending revival. The church had a congregation of 1000 members. Driving from out of town we arrived late, well after the service had commenced. As we made our way into the crowded sanctuary, we realized there were no empty seats. An usher led us up a stairway to a balcony where we found two vacant seats. Actually, these seats were "reserved". God had reserved them for us in answer to our prayers. We sat down. As we looked around we wondered what was transpiring for an eerie silence pervaded the sanctuary. Where was the preacher? We wondered why everyone was sitting in silence—it was obvious we had arrived well into the service. As we sat there I began to feel an overpowering presence. This presence was heavy, as if a heavy drape was coming down upon me. Suddenly, I felt an incredible desire to weep. Why I did not know. I fought the feeling until I glanced at my friend and noticed tears streaming down his face. I too began to weep. As I looked around me I noticed others weeping too. From the balcony, I looked down into the sanctuary and it was then I noticed that the choir members were passing a box of facial tissues back and forth between them. It seems they too were weeping.

Eventually, a teenager made his way down front and gave a testimony. When the whole event was over it was after ten o'clock. It was dark outside as my friend and I left for the parking lot. We recognized the pastor walking toward his car. We ran up to him and inquired what had taken place before we arrived. He told us, "I had a message to preach tonight, but God moved in so I just sat down and let the Holy Spirit run the service"

We asked, "What happened here tonight?"

The pastor was visibly exhausted. He slowly made his way to his car and turned and replied, "We're dead people. We are dead". Was all he offered.

"What? What do you mean?" I asked.

"We are dead people down here. We have died to ourselves. I cannot explain any better than that." With that he got in his car and drove off into the night.

As my friend and I stood beneath the moonlight on that hot Mississippi night, we just looked at each other obviously each perplexed at what we had just experienced. After making some phone calls to the church secretary the next day we learned what had transpired at this little church. It seemed earlier in the month there had been a men's retreat led by an African missionary. During this retreat the men of the church rededicated their lives to Christ and became new men. At home they treated their wives with a new respect and love. They read their Bibles and led in family devotions. Soon, the wives were so affected by this that they too had come down front to the church altar and confessed their sins and got right with God. Finally, (the evening we were there before we arrived) the teenagers had come down front and repented and many were saved. They had seen such a difference living in a true Christian home that they were impacted for Christ by their parent's behavior. Soon many others were brought to Christ in the surrounding neighborhood. Several months later the members of this little congregation pooled their financial resources and purchased the local abortion clinic and turned it into a Christian bookstore.

This is what accompanies revival: changed lives; new converts; joy unspeakable; and the powers of darkness pushed back. God builds his church with holy living stones and He receives all the glory.

When a church is run on the same lines as a circus, there may be crowds, but there is no Shekinah.

—Samuel Chadwick

Make a show; the people love a show, and you will gain the end of your ambition at once. The crowd is always ready for a sensation, and, alas, there are always those who are disposed to stimulate religion, to fill the churches by the method of sensationalism.

—W. Graham Scroggie

Because thou sayest, I am rich, and increased with goods, and have need of nothing; and knowest not that thou art wretched, and miserable, and poor, and blind, and naked.

—Revelation 3:17

Today the Christian Church is helpless. Behind the scenes and away from the public arena, we are facing powers of darkness too strong for us because somewhere in our personal lives we have forfeited all right to the Spirit's anointing, His authority and His power. In His absence all we can do is to substitute planning and organization, schemes and techniques.

—Alan Redpath

Chapter Eight

THE CAPPUCCINO CHURCH

"Take thou away from me the noise of thy songs: for I will not hear the melody of thy viols" (Amos 5:23).

In this chapter we will examine a trend in America which is disturbing and a major preventive to revival. Irreverence to God in churches handicaps the possibility of God visiting that church with revival. Things that grieve the Holy Spirit drive Him away. Unfortunately, there is a major movement in America among evangelical churches which has brought in the crowds but has grieved the heart of a Holy God. The "seeker service" has become popular but it is an abomination to God. Why such harsh words for a methodology which has had such success in the eyes of many churches? First, we would have to define success and ensuring that what the world views as success and what the Creator of the Universe views as success from His vantage point in eternity. Anyone can draw a crowd if the message spoken is appealing to the masses. The new paradigm in church growth is to follow this method of preaching an "unoffensive message" to get the crowds in. Be casual in attitude and dress. Have the music ape the world's latest trend. Show how God is a God of love. He loves everybody. It matters not that your lifestyle is an affront to Him—hey, he loves you anyway! All you have to do is come in and accept this loving God and then He will bless you while you are here on this earth and then He will bless you for all eternity. Never mention sin. Never bring up the term, "repentance". Preach a message that never brings up the subject of Christ crucified, much less about living a crucified life for Him. Don't ruffle the feathers. God just wants everybody to come in and have a big "party" with Him. Come on in. Have a cup of cappuccino and relax. Make some friends. Blasphemy! Dear brethren, why have we forsaken God for nickels and noses? Do we really believe that this is a standard of a New Testament church? Did the early apostles stop people on the streets of Rome and invite them in for some coffee, fellowship, and to listen to a message of a big hearted God? Did the Apostle Paul "water down" his message of Christ just to "pack them in" in Ephesus? Where are we going with this nonsense? Nowhere!

Being a church planter opened my eyes to the Christian community in which I live. As I visited churches to see what was "working" I was shocked beyond belief. What people are calling "church" in reality is just a fellowship gathering with some "light teaching" of God's Word. Here is an example of the "typical" worship service out there today: fun, fellowship, foolishness.

I will describe in detail a church service of a "Cappuccino Church" which I visited recently. I was greeted at the door (on a Sunday morning) by greeters wearing shorts and short sleeve shirts. There was a "coffee bar". The video screen was on ready for a power point message. The music was loud. Children were shouting and laughing in the sanctuary. Then the service began with the pastor informing the attendees that this coming Monday evening would be "Ladies Massage Night". At so and so's house a masseuse would arrive and give massages to the ladies of the church to relieve their stress. The pastor wore a short sleeve shirt as he addressed the assembly. Then the person leading the music called God a guy. He stated, (as he walked around strumming his guitar) "Wow! Just think, on a recent mission trip to Central America I realized that the same 'guy' I was serving down there was the same 'guy' I was serving up here!" Then they turned the decibel level up for the rock music.

My ears hurt for three days after this episode.

At another so-called church service in a different church altogether I heard a pastor comment, "Hey, you know what I would do if I won a million dollars? I would not give it away. I would buy a great big house and invite you all to come and we would have a huge party! We would party for God!" By the way his music was just as offensive only more elaborate. Never once in his message did he mention Calvary. Never once did he mention sin. Or forgiveness. Or repentance. He spoke only of how God was a loving God with a big heart. He might have mentioned Jesus once or twice in passing.

Where are we going with this garbage while people perish every day? We have left our standard of what church is. It is not a place to come and "have a good time", to listen to an easy message of happiness and comfort. It is not a place to come and laugh, to share a cup of coffee with a friend. If you want to do that, go to Starbucks or some other coffee shop. What church is in a biblical sense, is a place of prayer. A place of meeting a Holy God. A place of preaching Christ on a cross for the redemption of humankind and the glory of God. A place to sing hymns which make us holy—to seek God with a contrite heart and a humble head and to worship Him with thankful lips. A place where heaven touches man by experiencing a Holy God through a message preached by a holy man of God anointed with the Spirit of God. A place where the Holy Spirit convicts sinners of sin and shows them a gaping hell awaiting them unless they repent and accept Jesus Christ who died on a brutal cross for the remission of their sins. Yes, you can come and still have a donut and a cup of coffee while you wait for the service to begin. It is all right to laugh with a friend and have fellowship. But brethren. Let us keep the main thing the main thing! Don't follow a program just because it draws crowds and sells books and everybody else is doing it so it must be working. God's way is the narrow way. The broad way is the world's way.

Did you ever stop to think that New York City, the place which hosts all the godless theatrical shows, is called, "Broadway?" The world is the Broadway of life—entertainment, fun, and hedonism. The Christian way is one of dying to self, living for God, becoming like Jesus. How can we advance His kingdom when all our efforts are focused on advancing ours? Arise sleeping saints. Wake up slumbering church, while there is still time by the mercy of His grace and longsuffering of His patience. The world perishes while we play our little games. God have mercy on us!

There is in all things a good, a better, and a best. That is especially true in our spiritual life.
—A. B. Simpson

Life with a capital "L"—the vertical line of the L represents the life in contact with God; the horizontal line, the line in contact with our fellow men. This, then, is the best life, the Christian life—life with a capital "L".
—A. Lindsay Glegg

Let's get back to the "old time" religion.
—Vance Havner

We don't want revival; we want blessings.
—Leonard Ravenhill

Chapter Nine
GOD'S STANDARD

"And the Lord said unto me, Amos, what seest thou? And I said, A plumbline. Then said the Lord, behold, I will set a plumbline in the midst of my people Israel: I will not again pass by them anymore" (Amos 7:8).

In this chapter we will examine what hinders revival and how to lead a church to prepare their hearts for revival, how we can take our church through the process of praying for revival. One major element in a true revival is the presence of the Holy Spirit. Grieve Him away and the revival will end or not come at all. Things that hinder revival are listed below. This is not a comprehensive list by any means.

- Self righteousness
- Unconfessed and unrepented sin
- Humanism
- Worldliness
- Materialism
- An unforgiving heart toward others, including toward other Christians
- Pride
- False doctrine
- Rock music or irreverent music
- Lack of evangelism and the concern over lost souls
- Lack of mission focus or support for missionaries
- Holy huddles and cliques
- Sharing in God's glory

- Lack of reverence for a Holy God
- Hypocrites in the church — *isn't the church for sinners?*
- Boasting and bragging
- Gossip
- Lying
- Lack of prayer
- Watered down gospel message
- Ungodly pastor in the pulpit or ungodly staff members

Asking the Spirit of God to search the soul and shine His perfect searchlight on any sin in the believer will be a good starting point for any revival. Often revivals come after the persons praying for it end up publicly confessing their sins. What will be mentioned here in this chapter on preparing for revival does not in any way guarantee that revival will come to you and your church. God is sovereign and His visitations are heaven sent. However, He looks at the hearts of His people and He hears their prayers. What kind of environment fosters revival? What environment hinders it? Usually, (generally speaking) a congregation will reflect their pastor. If you are a holy man of God they, for the most part, should have a desire for holiness as well. If you are a praying pastor, your congregation should in turn have a heart for prayer. They follow you their leader. If your preaching is shallow your people will likely be shallow as well. If your preaching is deep and full of meat they will raise their heads up to follow you. If you are a pastor who deeply desires to see revival, then that feeling and desire will also be reflected in your congregation.

First and foremost, revivals are birthed from prayer and a confession of sins. Gather your congregation to pray both individually and corporately. Be a leader in this. Lead them in prayer. Be consistent. Institute a weekly prayer meeting where prayer is the focus—no preaching. Have them come in expectation to pray corporately. Hymns or songs may be sung but be careful in the selection of them. Make certain they are reverent to a Holy God. Here are some other useful suggestions:

- Set up a twenty four hour prayer chain with your congregation
- Gather some of your top men or staff to join you early in the morning to pray once or twice a week for an hour or two each day.
- Make sure your prayers are not self-centered or focused only on your church. Pray for missions and missionaries, the lost in your community, the sick, the imprisoned, and political leaders. Pray for the most wicked person in the community to be converted. Often in revivals this very thing occurs. The most reprobate are saved.
- Lead your members in prayer walks around neighborhoods. Pray over each house and bathe it in travailing prayer for conversions to occur.
- Begin a street preaching ministry that reaches the worst segment of your community. The drunks, the prostitutes, the down and out. Who else will reach them with the gospel if not you?
- Go into the wealthiest neighborhood in your community going door to door sharing the gospel. Normally, most ministers ignore this segment of the populace believing them to be too hard to reach because of their wealth. Rich people are just as hungry for God's Word as the poor—oftentimes more so. They realize the emptiness and futility of material things.
- Begin a preaching series on the holiness of God for a month or two. Then preach on hell next. Preach on the sinfulness of sin and what an offense it is to a holy God. Preach an entire series on heaven. On the judgement seat for believers. Get your congregation focused on eternity. Talk about their lives being wood, hay, and stubble; or gold, silver, and

precious stones.
- Preach an end time message from Revelation and show how short the time is before the Lord returns.
- Have an altar call in your church for believers to come and rededicate their lives to Christ.
- Encourage your church to memorize Scripture
- Become a church that is known as a "Praying Church"

Do you have to do all of the aforementioned? No. Revival is not a program or a methodology. The reason these things were even mentioned at all is to help you have a place to begin the process for revival. To awaken your church from the dullness of slumber. To get them on their knees and in their Bibles.

This leads us to the next chapter in which we will focus on experiencing personal revival. How can you lead your people in revival without being revived yourself?

Prayer is never rejected so long as we do not cease to pray. The chief failure of prayer is its cessation.

—P. T. Forsyth

The noblest, the grandest, the boldest, the most magnificent act a human can perform on this earth is to pray.

—Alexander Whyte

The habit of regular, lingering prayer, more than anything else, makes any Christian a dangerously holy weapon in the hand of God.

—J. Sidlow Baxter

I waited patiently for the LORD; and he inclined unto me, and heard my cry.

—Psalm 40:1

Chapter Ten

REND YOUR HEART

"And rend your heart, and not your garments, and turn unto the Lord your God" (Joel 2:13).

This could very well be the most important chapter in the book. For what is more important than one's own relationship with God? As with Adam in the garden, God desires to fellowship with us on a personal and intimate basis. He desires a love relationship with His bride. In many instances we fail here. And if not with outright unfaithfulness and adultery on our part, then at least our love wanes toward Him when it should be the very opposite.

Why does our love wane? Often times we mistakenly think that activity and busyness in serving Him is our way of showing our love for Him. Our Christian service is indeed an outflow of our love toward Him; however, to replace an intimate love relationship with a hectic schedule of service spells death in a relationship. If you say you love your spouse and seldom spend time with her, if she is last on your priority list, how do you show your affection toward her? Well, you might say that you are working and by working you are clothing, feeding, and providing for her survival. And so you justify your busyness and your neglect of her. We do the same terrible thing to God. We work for Him tirelessly; we travel here and there for Him, we do this and that for Him, and our busy activity is a surrogate way for us to show our love for Him.

I once heard a preacher tell this story and it was extremely effective in getting its message across. It seems this man grew up on a farm in the South. As a boy he had a dog, not an expensive breed—just a mutt. But he loved the mutt and the mutt loved him. When he awoke in the summertime, the boy would rush outside early in the morning to ride his bike with his dog running beside him. Every day when the boy would step out onto the porch of his house there the dog would be patiently and expectantly waiting for him. The dog would smile when he saw his friend. And the boy would smile when he greeted and patted his faithful friend. Together they would ride and run through the woods and across the meadows thoroughly enjoying one another's companionship.

One day the boy went outside to the porch and the dog was gone. At first he assumed the dog was already preoccupied with hunting a rabbit or a bird, and that he would return later. However, the next sunrise had a disappointment for the boy, as he realized the dog was not there, nor was he ever coming back. He had either become lost or killed (at least that is what the boy's father told him). Still, every day the boy got up from his bed and with a hopeful heart peered outside the screen porch to see if the dog was there waiting for him. Finally, he realized the dog was gone.

This minister then made the application to the congregation. He said that it had broken his heart when he lost his dog. He grieved over him on a daily basis. And as he told the story he still had a tear in his eye and a broken voice. You see, we are like the boy. Every day God waits for us to spend time with him in a love relationship. He anticipates that fellowship. He desires to spend quality time with us in a loving way. What do we do? We rush outside to the porch, briefly pat him on the head (by granting him five or ten minutes in prayer before we rush out to our day) and then off we go to ride our bike without him. Oh, we are riding our bike for Him. We are busy for Him here and busy for Him there. We seldom realize we left Him back on the porch. Worse than that is this application: God is the boy and we are the dog. He comes outside everyday to see his friend but we never even show up! He longs for us and we are not there. We are gone in our busyness. Preacher, fellow Christian worker, take heed to this message. We have left our first love as the church in Ephesus. That is why we have no power. When we preach, it is merely doctrine dressed up and it has no life changing effect to its hearers. This generation is the most educated, lettered, bunch of ministers than ever before, and what have we got? Swollen heads and shrunken hearts. We make an attempt to tell others about the love of God when we ourselves are mere babies on the topic in a relational sense.

The average pastor spends ten minutes a day in prayer. Shameful! Worse than that, it is criminal! For it is a crime against a Holy God to forsake Him as we do in the name of Christian service. How He longs for us to be with Him! How can He ever make us like His dear Son if we refuse to spend any time with Him? Brethren, get on your knees right now and confess your lack of love and lack of time spent with this faithful Friend. Ask the Holy Spirit to break your heart in this matter.

In the next chapter we will look at how to have a productive quiet time.

And in very deed for this cause have I raised thee up, for to shew in thee my power; and that my name may be declared throughout all the earth.

—Exodus 9:16

Anoint me with your Spirit, Lord, for this strategic hour; that I may preach your holy word, with consecrated power.

—Stephen F. Olford

All the resources of the Godhead are at our disposal!

—Jonathan Goforth

There is pow'r, pow'r, wonder working pow'r, in the blood of the Lamb.

—Lewis E. Jones

Chapter Eleven

POWER WITH GOD

"And in the morning, rising up a great while before day, he went out, and departed into a solitary place, and there prayed" (Mark 1:35).

It was a habit with Jesus to rise early and spend time with the Father. If this was the pattern for Jesus Christ during His earthly ministry, why do we fail here so miserably? In all we do in the name of God, this is where we fail the most. The disciples asked Jesus, "Lord teach us to pray". They had witnessed Him praying like this on a regular basis. They saw His power. They wanted it! Before He ascended, He told them to wait in Jerusalem for the Holy Spirit to clothe them with power. Why do we miss this lesson? The main reason we lack power in the pulpit is our lack of prayer and vital relationship with Him!

Great men of faith such as John Wesley, George Whitefield, and a host of others were all early risers. The Bible commentator, Albert Barnes, wrote his *Barnes' Notes* mainly before daybreak. J. Sidlow Baxter rose at 5 a.m. every day of his life (except when he reached his 90's. From age 90 to 96 he rose at 6 a.m.). George Whitefield had just finished dinner at a nobleman's manse and the host leaned back in his chair and turned the topic of conversation to recreation. Whitefield excused himself by saying it was 9 p.m. and he had to leave for he had an early morning appointment at 4 a.m.. The nobleman asked who on earth would be meeting with him at 4 a.m. and Whitefield replied—"God".

It has been reported that the average pastor spends ten minutes a day in prayer. Is it a wonder we have prayerless congregations? Is it a wonder that we lack power? The most vital aspect of a Christian's life is his or her prayer life! If we are derelict in this we are derelict everywhere. How can we attempt to know the heart of God without prayer? How can we lead others without being led ourselves? How can we mortify the deeds of the body without first standing in His holy presence at the beginning of the day? Brethren, this lack of prayer in your life, in your church, is the reason you lack power from on High. It is high time we stand against all this man-centered philosophy of Christianity today and get down to business with a Holy God!

A man's walk with God is as deep as his prayer life. If you are shallow here (and shame on you) you are shallow everywhere—I don't care how lettered you are and how much you have achieved academically. The main reason pulpits lack power today is the messenger himself lacks power! He is like Samson who left the tent of Delilah and shook himself not knowing the Spirit of the Lord had left him. When will we stop following programs and formulas and follow Christ Himself! The Spirit of God is grieved beyond measure by our intellectual and humanistic approach to the things of God! We run back and forth from conference to conference and read the new "hot" Christian bestseller to get our guidance. We are no more effective than a mouse aimlessly running through a maze with no chance of getting out. If we are going to break out for God and the benefit of humankind let us get serious in this matter of prayer. When we stand at the Bema Seat and Jesus reviews the montage of our lives in the most minute detail, many professional Christians will weep over the painful reality that they seldom prayed—much less prayed with the proper motive.

So let us get down to business. If you do not want to get serious with God then skip this chapter and give this book away to someone who does. There is no hope for you as a fruit bearing Christian if you have little desire for prayer. You yourself need prayer. You are as dead as this printed bark.

For those who wish to go forward with God, let us proceed cautiously for we are treading on holy ground.

Stephen Olford wrote a booklet entitled, *Manna In The Morning*. I highly recommend it, for it is Stephen Olford who impacted me more than any other man on the necessity of having a "Quiet Time". In this little booklet, Dr. Olford begins by stating, "The first hour of your day is by far the biggest". He then lays out the pattern to be used for an effective Quiet Time with God. It is as follows:

1. A definite time and place
2. A good-sized, easily read Bible
3. A prayer list or prayer cycle
4. A personal notebook
5. A spirit of expectancy

Because of Stephen Olford, I have had an effective quiet time for the past twelve years. For it is only possible to know the heart of God by spending time with God—praying and studying His Word. How I approach my time with the Lord in the morning is this way: I do not use this time just to study His word or to merely pray over a list of prayer needs. The primary object of my quiet time is to MEET GOD. To climb into His presence by the blood of His Son and the enabling of His Spirit. He desires to fellowship with me and YOU! He loves us so deeply that it breaks His heart when we fail to show up for that divine appointment. There is grave danger in being callous in this area of our Christian walk. We will pay dearly for the lack of this time spent in communion with God, not only while here temporarily on the sod of earth, but in the halls of heaven. Sidlow Baxter used to say, "Now is the time for us to pray, pray, pray". This is the only way to personal revival and the only way to maintain it!

If Christ waited to be anointed before He went to preach, no young man ought to preach until he, too, has been anointed by the Holy Ghost.

—F. B. Meyer

We need God-called men who will take the book of God and preach the Son of God with the anointing of the Spirit of God.

—Adrian Rogers

Church strength does not consist in its numbers and its money, but in the holiness of its members. Church strength is not found in these worldly attachments or endowments, but in the endowment of the Holy Spirit.

—E. M. Bounds

In the morning, felt exceeding dead to the world and all its enjoyments.

—David Brainerd

Chapter Twelve
POWER IN THE PULPIT

"But ye shall receive power, after that the Holy Ghost is come upon you: and ye shall be witnesses unto me both in Jerusalem, and in Samaria, and unto the uttermost part of the earth" (Acts 1:8).

There is no shortage of churches in America. There is an abundance of preachers. In many instances churches have more money today than ever before in history. We can say of ourselves, "We lack nothing". Yet we lack the most vital thing necessary to bring men to Christ; we lack power—power from on high. D. L. Moody realized this when two women from his Chicago church confronted him after a service and informed him that his messages were lacking power. At first he was offended. Then, while in New York City, alone in a room, he sought God and had a breakthrough. From that point forward his ministry had a new dimension—an anointing which he brought in power to England and thousands were converted. To understand this power, this holy unction, we will look at a conversion which occurred in England under Moody's preaching. It is the personal testimony of C. T. Studd regarding his father's conversion.

> My father was just a man of the world, loving all sorts of worldly things. He had made a fortune in India and had come back to England to spend it. He was very fond of sports of all kinds. He would go into regular training that he might go fox hunting, but above all he was an enthusiast

on horse racing. He was passionately fond of horses to begin with and when he saw fine horses he would buy them and train them, and then he would race them. He had a large place in the country, where he made a race course, and he won the biggest steeple-chase in London three times. At last he got hold of a horse better than anyone he had ever had, and so certain was he of winning the race that he wrote to a friend in London and said, "If you are a wise man you will come to the race tomorrow and put every penny you have on my horse".

Unknown to my father this man had been converted. Mr. Moody had come to England and had been preaching. Nobody believed very much at that time in a man getting up to preach the gospel unless he had two things—the title of Reverend, and a white tie round his neck. The papers could not understand such a preacher as Mr. Moody, who had neither, and of course they printed column after column against him. But they could not help seeing that he could get more people to his meetings than half a dozen archbishops, and that more were converted than by twenty ordinary ministers. Of course they did not put the right construction on things. They said that Mr. Sankey had come over to sell organs, and Mr. Moody to sell his hymn books. My father read the papers day after day and these things tickled him immensely. I remember one evening he threw the paper down and said, "Well, anyhow, when this man comes to London I am going to hear him. There must be some good about the man or he would never be abused so much by the papers".

Well, father went up to London the next day according to promise, and met his friend. This man had been over to Ireland when Mr. Moody was there, and as he was about to leave Dublin had missed his train. God was even in that, missing a train. It was Saturday night, and the man had to remain over Sunday. As he was looking about the streets that evening he saw the big bills advertising Moody and Sankey, and he thought, "I will just go and hear those Americans". He went and God met him; he went again and God converted him. He was a new man, and yet when my father wrote that letter he never said anything about it. When they met and drove along in a carriage father talked of nothing but horses, and told this man if he were a wise man he would put up every penny he had on that horse. After father had finished his business he came back to this friend and said, "How much money have you put on my horse?" "Nothing." My father said, "You are the biggest fool I ever saw; didn't I tell you what a good horse he was? But though you are a fool, come along with me to dinner". After dinner my father said, "Now, where shall we go to amuse ourselves?" His friend said, "Anywhere". My father said, "Well, you are the guest; you shall choose where we shall go". "Well, we will go and hear Moody." My father said, "Oh, no, this isn't Sunday. We will go to the theater, or concert". But the man said, "You promised to go wherever I chose", So my father had to go. They found the building was full and there were no seats in the hall except special ones. This man knew he would never get my father there again, so he worked himself into the crowd until he came across one of the committee. He said to him, "Look here; I have brought a wealthy sporting gentleman here, but I will never get him here again if we do not get a seat". The man took them in and put them right straight in front of Mr. Moody. My father never took his eyes off Mr. Moody until he finished his address. After the meeting my father said, "I will come and hear this man again. He just told me everything I had ever done". My father kept going until he was soundly converted.

That afternoon my father had been full of a thing that takes possession of a man's heart and head more than anything else—that passion for horse racing; and in the evening he was a changed man. It was the same skin, but a new man altogether inside. When we boys came home from college we didn't understand what had come over him, but father kept continually telling us that he was born again. We thought he was just born upside down, because he was always asking us about our souls, and we didn't like it. Of course, he took us to hear Mr. Moody, and we were impressed a good deal, but were not converted.

When my father was converted of course he could not go on living the same life as before. He could not go to balls, card parties, and all that sort of thing. His conscience told him so, and he said to Mr. Moody: "I want to be straight with you. If I become a Christian will I have to give up racing, and shooting, and hunting, and theaters, and balls?" "Well", Mr. Moody said, "Mr. Studd, you have children and people you love; and now you are a saved man yourself, and you want to get them saved. God will give you some souls and as soon as ever you have won a soul you won't care about any of the other things". Sure enough, we found to our astonishment that father didn't care for any of those things any longer; he only cared about one thing, and that was saving souls.

He took us to hear Mr. Moody and other men, and when Mr. Moody left England my father opened his country house, and held meetings there in the evenings. He asked ministers and business men from London to come down and speak to the people about their souls. The people would come for miles to attend the meetings, and many were converted.

The story goes on to say that it was at these meetings where C. T. Studd was converted himself. If anyone is familiar with the mission work in China (and later Africa) where God used C. T. Studd, it would doubly add to the power of this story. How could a man of the world like Studd's father, who had all the money he could ever spend, end up changing his course of life so dramatically? Obviously the Spirit of God got hold of him in the Moody meetings. But let us not miss the importance of this related story; if Moody had been just an ordinary preacher with no anointing upon him, do you believe Studd's father would have been saved at those meetings? Be careful how you answer. I am not implying that God cannot use ordinary men, quite the opposite. Ordinary men are the ones he is looking for. However, it is when he takes an ordinary man and anoints that vessel with His power of the Holy Spirit—then and only then does the work of God take place. Well, you say, my church is full each week and I have a large ministry and I disagree with what you are implying. Fine. Let eternity decide how successful your earthly ministry was. For God does not hand out heavenly rewards based on the how the world views success. Many ministries that appear to be complete failures on the outside are often huge successes in the realm of eternity. Everything God does is upside down to what we think is successful.

In the next chapter we will continue to look at power in the pulpit and how your church may be transformed.

*If the Holy Spirit does not come, and give
spiritual life, we may preach until we have not
another breath left, but we shall not raise from
the tomb of sin even the soul of a little child,
or bring a single sinner to the feet of Christ.*
                                            —C. H. Spurgeon

*I received many blows and wounds; one
was particularly large and near my temples.*
                                            —George Whitefield

*I am come here this day, and would not
change my lot with the greatest in the world.
I lay down my life willingly and cheerfully for
Christ and His cause, and I heartily forgive
all mine enemies. I forgive all them who
gave me my sentence, and them who were
the chief cause of my taking; and I forgive
him who is behind me (the executioner). I
advise you who are the Lord's people, to
be sincere in the way of godliness, and
you who know little or nothing of the power
thereof, to come to Him.*
                              —John Dick upon the scaffold at the
                                     Grassmarket in Edinburgh

*I can't. God never said I could. He can. He
always said He would.*
                                            —Major W. Ian Thomas

Chapter Thirteen
POWER OF PENTECOST

"And suddenly there came a sound from heaven as of a rushing mighty wind, and it filled all the house where they were sitting. And there appeared unto them cloven tongues like as of fire, and it sat upon each of them" (Acts 2:3-4).

Church activity today is often confused for the smile of heaven. We look at a church and on the outside it appears healthy and growing and prosperous. And many are. But not all of them are in the eyes of a Holy God. Oftentimes, the Spirit of God has long left the church and the church is completely unaware of His absence. We see people come in and make professions for Christ yet the community in which we live is seldom changed in the light of heaven. Why is this? We are trained, educated, sincere, and hard workers—often worked too hard. Why do we lack power? Let us take you to a man by the name of Samuel Chadwick, a former principal at Cliff College in Sheffield, England. Let us look at what he wrote back in 1932 for it has relevance for today.

> The Spirit has never abdicated His authority nor relegated His power. ... Any church that is man-managed instead of God-governed is doomed to failure. A minister that is college-trained but not Spirit-filled works no miracles. The church that multiplies committees and neglects prayer may be fussy, noisy, enterprising, but it labors in vain and spends its strength for naught. It is

possible to excel in mechanics and fail in dynamic. There is a superabundance of machinery; what is wanting is power. To run an organization needs no God. Man can supply the energy, enterprise, and enthusiasm for things human. The real work of a church depends upon the power of the Spirit.

The presence of the Spirit is vital and central to the work of the church. Nothing else avails. Apart from Him wisdom becomes folly, and strength weakness. The church is called to be a "spiritual house" and a holy priesthood. Only spiritual people can be its "living stones", and only the Spirit-filled its priests.

Scholarship is blind to spiritual truth till He reveals. Worship is idolatry till He inspires. Preaching is powerless if it be not a demonstration of His power. Prayer is vain unless He energizes. Human resources of learning and organization, wealth and enthusiasm, reform and philanthropy, are worse than useless if there be no Holy Ghost in them. The Church always fails at the point of self-confidence. When a church is run on the same lines as a circus, *there may be crowds, but there is no Shekinah* (emphasis mine).

Does this not illustrate the majority of us today? Crowds, noise, celebration, blowing horns, and absolutely no power! This is why we can have churches on every corner in our land and still make no difference to the moral downgrade in society. In a true revival (history has shown us) there is change within the community: taverns close, gambling ceases, often the worst sinners in town are saved. People flock to the church not only to hear the Word of God but to meet the God of the Word. To worship Him. To adore Him. To fall on their faces in thanksgiving for extending them good grace to see how wicked and vile they really were apart from Him. George Whitefield used to tell the thronging thousands who came to hear him as he preached in fields beneath a sky above him, "Listen sinners, you're monsters, monsters of iniquity! You deserve Hell! And the worst of your crimes is that criminals though you've been, you haven't had the good grace to see it!" He said, "If you will not weep for your sins and your crimes against a Holy God, George Whitefield will weep for you!" That man would put his head back and he would sob like a baby. Why? Because they were in danger of hell? No! But because they were monsters of iniquity, that didn't even see their sin or care about their crimes.

We lack power in the pulpit for many reasons. We fear the audience for our reputations. We do not wish to offend anyone with truth. So we water it down here and there. We tell sinners that they really aren't all that bad but a good God can save them. We seldom ever preach on Hell much less the Judgement Seat of Christ. Oh we read a news item in the paper and then build our sermon around it for a "topical study" on morality. The apostle Paul declared, *"For the preaching of the cross is to them that perish foolishness; but unto us which are saved it is the power of God" (1 Cor. 1:18).* We preach culture instead of the cross! What we need today, in a time where God is being legislated out of our country by the humanistic courts and where true Christians are a minority (which has been the case in history), are more ministers who are not afraid to preach the inerrant Word of God. This cannot be better described than in the words of the well-known preacher and Bible teacher, Dr. Adrian Rogers. He said, "We need God-called men who will take the Book of God and preach the Son of God with the anointing of the Spirit of God. We need men with warm hearts, wet eyes, clear heads, and tongues aflame".

If any one is familiar with the ministry of Adrian Rogers, they know full well the aforementioned can be said of him.

His church by the way has a membership of over 30,000. It is standing proof that one does not have to water down the truth to attract crowds.

Why are we afraid to offend people by preaching truth? Could it be (in some cases) that our profession has become just that; a job, a career choice, where we are dependent on the steady paycheck and we will do nothing to put that financial security in jeopardy? Are we afraid to put our retirement plan at risk? Preach the truth brethren, at any cost! We will be held accountable for how we handle the Word of God. God will deal with us more severely than most because we are the messengers of God. If we desire true power in the pulpit and in our churches, this is a good beginning.

Why sleep ye? Rise and pray, lest ye enter into temptation.

—Luke 22:46

In 1740 when God moved through New England it was called "The Great Awakening". Revival has often been referred to as "an awakening". At Gethsemane Jesus faced the "crisis point" of His earthly ministry and His disciples slept right through it. Today the church is in a "crisis point" and we are sleeping right through it.

—E. A. Johnston

When there is a worldly spirit in the church, there is need of revival. The Church is clearly backslidden when Christians conform to the world in dress and attitudes, seeking worldly entertainment ... it shows they are far from God and need awakening.

—Charles G. Finney

He became a crucified Christ that He might have crucified followers.

—F. J. Huegel

Chapter Fourteen

ASLEEP IN A HAILSTORM

"But the Lord sent out a great wind into the sea, and there was a mighty tempest in the sea, so that the ship was like to be broken. ... But Jonah was gone down into the sides of the ship; and he lay, and was fast asleep" (Jonah 1:4-5).

(This chapter is dedicated to the memory of Len Ravenhill).

Can there be a better comparison to today's ministers than this passage from the word of God? Are we not asleep while the storm rages around us? Have we not run from the direct commands of God—the commands to preach Christ and Him crucified, the commands to live a holy life. Are we running from God ourselves much like poor Jonah? Will God in His mercy have to cast us and our ministries into the foaming waves to get our attention? I pray not—but it may take this to awaken us. How can we lead others to Christ when we ourselves have no inkling of who we are in Christ?

Instead of professionalism, what we need today is brokenness before Him.

Instead of memorized prayers, heart cries.

Instead of dry doctrine with no heart, wet eyes and a broken heart.

Instead of pride backed by academic degrees, humility upon our knees.

Instead of new buildings and more ballfields, street preaching on corners and mission fields.

Instead of easy believeism during gospel invitations, we

need repentance and consecration.

Instead of living to please self and enjoy life, dying to self and living the crucified life.

Instead of preaching with no power, incarnate preaching with Holy Spirit power.

Brethren, until we are willing to do the aforementioned, we will lack power from on high and our ministries will never be what heaven desires them to be. We will be as Samuel Chadwick stated so aptly in the previous chapter, "there may be crowds, but there is no Shekinah". In today's dull thinking, a ministry's success is judged by the standard of the world—money, fame, crowds—when in the light of heaven, these are in reality wood, hay, stubble. When will we awaken from our slumber? One way is to experience personal revival. If your ministry has become merely routine minus passion, if your prayer time has become one of "dry eyes", if you have forsaken your first love, if you have been relying more on self than relying on the Lord and crucifying self; then this next chapter is for you. We will focus on how to take the pathway to personal revival.

God is looking for a man who will throw himself entirely on God. Whenever self-effort, self-glory, self-seeking or self-promotion enters into the work of revival, then God leaves us to ourselves.

—Ted S. Rendall

Go ye, inquire of the LORD for me, and for the people, and for all Judah, concerning the words of this book that is found: for great is the wrath of the LORD that is kindled against us, because our fathers have not hearkened unto the words of this book, to do according unto all that which is written concerning us.

—2 Kings 22:13

He leadeth me, He leadeth me, By His own hand He leadeth me.

— Joseph H. Gilmore

Be thou my Vision, O Lord of my heart; naught be all else to me save that thou art;

—Irish Hymn, 8th Century

Chapter Fifteen
A NEW HEART

"Create in me a clean heart, O God; and renew a right spirit within me. Cast me not away from thy presence; and take not thy holy spirit from me. Restore unto me the joy of thy salvation; and uphold me with thy free spirit. Then I will teach transgressors thy ways; and sinners shall be converted unto thee" (Ps. 51:10-13).

King David knew this topic well. He had experienced true revival. His glaring disobedience to the things of God and his ensuing, deceitful cover-up made him dull to spiritual things. I would venture to say his fellowship with God during this sad interval in his life was at an all-time low. Oh, he still performed the kingly duties in the name of the Lord. On the outside his entire kingdom (with the exception of a select few) saw no change in him. He still smiled when he addressed them. He still performed dutifully the requirements of running a kingdom. But his kingdom had cracks within it so deep that soon it would give away under him like a dark sinkhole. Yes, God forgave David when he repented of his sins and turned back to the Creator. Yet, as all who willingly sin find out, he had to live with the consequences of his sin the rest of his natural days.

The Bible has lessons for us to learn. It warns of the dangers of adultery, the judgement of God upon sin; it also provides a way for a sheep who has strayed to return to the Good Shepherd. God in his mercy provided His Son Jesus for the remission of our sins at Calvary's cross. Through the atoning blood we may appropriate access to the throne of God. The entire process of personal revival hinges on the door frame of forgiveness. How can we truly be used of God if our hearts are far from Him in sin. Let us call our lack of love for Him what it is—SIN! We sin against light given to us by His revealed Word and the illumination of His Holy Spirit. Look what the priests did during the revival under Hezekiah, *"And they gathered their brethren, and sanctified themselves, and came, according to the commandment of the king, by the words of the LORD, to cleanse the house of the LORD. And the priests went into the inner part of the house of the LORD, to cleanse it, and brought out all the uncleanness that they found in the temple of the LORD into the court of the house of the LORD. And the Levites took* it, *to carry* it *out abroad into the brook Kidron"* (2 Chron. 29:15-16).

Relating this passage to us, God is telling us that unless we are willing to "clean house" and get right with Him, He will not honor our work. Cleaning our house is twofold:

1. Clean the temple
    Notice in the passage the word "it" is emphasised. This is to draw attention to the idols which had profaned the temple, the unclean things. It is time that we, as priests of God, clean the temples of our sanctuaries of the filth and abominations to the Lord. This could fall into several categories: ungodly music (rock music is an example of ungodly music), neglecting to preach truth, not showing sinners the true way to the cross, lack of holiness in the messenger.

2. Clean the temple of our heart
    King David had neglected to do this and it cost him dearly. Until we seek Him in contriteness, with wet eyes and a fervent heart He will not reward us. For *"he is a rewarder of them that diligently seek him"* (Heb. 11:6). Hezekiah realized this. *"And he did that which was right in the sight of the LORD, according to all that David his father had done"* (2 Chron. 29:2).
    He brought the priests and the Levites and gathered

them together into the east street and told them, *"Hear me, ye Levites, sanctify now yourselves, and sanctify the house of the LORD God of your fathers, and carry forth the filthiness out of the holy place" (2 Chron. 29:5).*

Are we willing to do the same? Weigh carefully what this wise twenty-five year old king said. He ordered them to do two things: 1. Sanctify yourselves. 2. Sanctify the house of the LORD. Brethren, God will NOT visit us and manifest Himself to us with the power of Pentecost upon our church and ministry until we DO THESE TWO THINGS!

The end result of the actions of King Hezekiah were this: *"Then Hezekiah the king rose early, and gathered the rulers of the city, and went up to the house of the LORD" (v. 20).* In other words, the temple worship was restored! Did you get it? When we do these two things, sanctify ourselves and sanctify the house of the Lord, then we will have a breakthrough with heaven and true worship will be restored! We will see His glory. We will bow in reverent awe. We will sing praises and cry, "Hosanna!"

I once knew a brother minister who had been unkindly treated by some members of his flock and had fallen into a spirit of deep resentment. ... There fell upon him a spirit of prayer for his bitter enemies, and he found himself irresistibly pouring his heart to God for them. Then he was prompted by a deep desire to return to his people, whom he had left for a time under a sense of injury. As he finished his morning service, the first persons to greet him were the two brethren that had so grievously wronged him. To his surprise they hastened forward with the most cordial welcome, and the reconciliation that followed was deep and lasting. ... The moment his own heart had gotten right, God made all the other things right.

—A. B. Simpson

Forgiveness is God's command.

—Martin Luther

There is a golden thread that weaves its way through revivals and if this purified thread is broken it has been a bar to revival throughout history; to which I refer to the golden thread of a forgiving heart toward others. When one researches the history of revival it is plainly shown that many revivals began accompanied by a sudden manifestation of God's presence, when Christians began to confess their sins of an unforgiving heart to one another.

—E. A. Johnston

But if ye forgive not men their trespasses, neither will your Father forgive your trespasses.

—Matthew 6:15

Chapter Sixteen

THE PROCESS OF REVIVAL

"Return to Me, declares the Lord Almighty, and I will return to you" (Zech. 1:3).

A good place to start the revival process was described in the previous chapter. How can we begin anew with our walk with the Lord? Return to Him. Return to His ways. Return to His Word. Let us begin with a personal survey. This is unlike the survey you take while walking through the shopping mall and are accosted by an individual with a dour face. Rather, this survey will be conducted by the Holy Spirit. Because if you wish to walk this path, you may not enter therein without the scorching searchlight of the Holy Spirit upon your ministry and personal life. For God is holy. He tells us clearly and warns us dramatically, *"Be ye clean, that bear the vessels of the Lord"* (Isa. 52:11). Are we living holy lives? Are we living up to the command, in Ephesians 1:4, *"that we should be holy and without blame before him in love"?* He called us not for our own self enjoyment but TO BE HOLY.

Take the following survey beneath the prayerful guidance of the Holy Spirit:

1. How much time do I spend in private prayer each day?
2. How much time do I spend in reading my Bible each day?
3. How much time do I spend in worshiping my God each day?

Now add up that time. Be honest and do not cheat—God is watching you. Did you do it? Having done this do you feel good about yourself or bad? Depending on how you answer, you may still require prayer! Sadly, it is reported that most ministers spend only ten minutes in prayer each day. Please do not brag if you spent twenty or a half hour. One of the translators of the King James Bible began each day by spending three hours in private prayer.

Now for part two in the survey. For this section add up the weekly time:

1.   How much time do you spend watching television or surfing the internet?
2.   How much time do you spend on your favorite hobby or sport?
3.   How much time do you spend frivolously?

Are you getting my point? Let us continue, however painful this process may be.

1.   Do you have a family altar in your home? (Family devotions)
     Yes ❑   No ❑

2.   When you pray, is it mainly for your ministry and yourself?
     Yes ❑   No ❑

3.   Do you pray for holiness and Christlikeness?
     Yes ❑   No ❑

Remember there should be no excuses here. In prayer remember that Job had a breakthrough when he eventually prayed for others.

1.   Do you perform your Christian duties out of habit or out of love?
     Habit ❑   Love ❑

2. Do you have dry eyes when you pray or wet eyes?
Dry Eyes ❑   Wet Eyes ❑

3. Do you have a concern over the lost?
None ❑   Some Concern ❑   Great concern ❑

Keep going, you can do it! Gut it out and continue.

1. Can you say of your ministry that it has fruit that remains and multiplies?
Yes ❑   No ❑

2. Do you hear God's voice as He leads you through your life?
Infrequently ❑   Frequently ❑

3. Would your spouse say of you that you are the same at home as in the church?
Yes ❑   No ❑

This test is something between you and God. Be honest please.

1. Do you have an accountability partner?
Yes ❑   No ❑

2. When you preach can you say that "virtue has left me"?
Yes ❑   No ❑

3. Do you seek the face of God when preparing sermons or do you turn to your favorite commentary?
God ❑   Commentary ❑

You are doing great! Keep going!

1. Are you living the first half of Ephesians (our wealth in

Christ)?   Yes ❑   No ❑

2. Are you living the second half of Ephesians (our walk in Christ)?   Yes ❑   No ❑

3. Do you worry about your reputation among your brethren? Yes ❑   No ❑

You are almost finished. Hang in there for the last lap.

1. Can people say of you after you preach, "It was as if he were in God's presence with God's message"? Sometimes ❑   No times ❑

2. Have you ever had a personal revival? Yes ❑   No ❑

3. Have you ever witnessed revival? Yes ❑   No ❑

The pain is over. Pray. Get alone. Seek Him who knows your heart better than yourself. You can become everything He wants you to become! We are more of a hindrance than the devil. Have a spiritual breakout for God! In turn, you will take your congregation along with you on the crest of the waves!

I would strongly suggest visiting a Spiritual Workshop if you cannot do this on your own. One which I can wholeheartedly recommend is one in which I experienced personal revival—I cannot express in words the benefit I received from Olford Ministries Intl. (Box 757800, Memphis, Tn 38175-7800, 901-757-7977, or www.olford.org). The institutes are life changing and ministry transforming; they have the best teaching for preachers that I know of. Give them a call. Or ask the Lord to guide you elsewhere. Whatever you decide, seek Him with a holy passion and He will never let you go or ever give you up!

We will continue to seek Him by looking at how we preach in the next chapter.

I am afraid I must say, to the great majority of the ministers even of the present day I think that their practical views of preaching the Gospel, whatever their theological views may be, are very defective indeed; and that their want of unction, and of the power of the Holy Ghost, is a radical defect in their preparation for the ministry.

—Charles G. Finney

No man has a right to speak for God who has no personal, firsthand knowledge of Him: he certainly will not speak with power.

—Samuel Chadwick

We believe such revival wonders can take place only as the Holy Spirit energizes the Word of God as it is preached. Genuine blessings cannot come unless the Holy Spirit energizes and convinces and stirs the people of God.

—A. W. Tozer

I asked them to come and talk with me, and they poured out their hearts in prayer that I might receive the filling of the Holy Spirit. There came a great hunger into my soul. I did not know what it was. I began to cry out as I never did before. I really felt that I did not want to live if I could not have this power for service.

—D. L. Moody

Chapter Seventeen

UNCTION—DO YOU HAVE IT?

"And she said, The Philistines be upon thee, Samson. And he awoke out of his sleep, and said, I will go out as at other times before, and shake myself. And he wist not that the Lord was departed from him" (Judg. 16:20).

Samson had the power. He slew a lion and thirty men, caught 300 foxes (try it sometime), and slew 1000 men with a mere jaw bone of an ass. Then what happened? Well, I guess you know the story. He was bound by new ropes of the world—the lust of the world and the pride of life. He got a hair cut and then he got his eyes put out. And then, only then, did he get humility.

In this chapter we will discuss unction. But first, examine the main barrier to it—pride. Do you boast about your successes like Samson did? Are you proud of the mass of people who flock to hear and see you? Are you self-satisfied with your ministry? Are you? Are you proud of the letters after your name? It is all right to take pride in one's achievements—I'm not talking about that. You know what I am talking about. You may have the smallest congregation, the largest congregation, the smallest Sunday school class, the largest Sunday school class. But do you have it? Unction, that is. When Jesus was walking through the crowd and the woman with the issue of blood touched Him he turned and said, *"Who touched my clothes?"* The verse reads, *"And Jesus, immediately knowing in himself that virtue had gone out of him, turned him about in the press, and said, Who touched my clothes?"* (Mark 5:30). The disciples did not understand Him. They had no clue what He was talking about. Do you? I have known men, great men of God, who when they preach, virtue leaves them. Why are they great men of God? Why has God used them so? They understood this passage and they understood the holy anointing of God upon his messengers.

The greatest crime in the church is humanism. Humanism has taken over Christianity. It is now popular to pay attention to what "man does". What man has to say. All of our programming is geared toward humanism. We must break free from this satanic stronghold in our churches or we will fail miserably until He returns.

The Bible has always had its enemies. Roman emperors, rulers, magistrates, Gnosticism, Neoplatonism, Montanism, popes, kings, presidents, Modernism, Liberalism, Higher Criticism, Supreme Court judges, atheism, feminism, communism, materialism, and relativism. But above all these the most deadly has been the rise of humanism. The dictionary definition of humanism is, "A system of thought that centers on humans and their values, capacities, and worth". So humanism is a system whose primary focus is man. The happiness of man. Seems harmless does it not? Applied to Christianity it is dangerous for it takes God out of the equation and makes man the center rather than God. Let us look at another dictionary definition: humanoid, "Having human characteristics or form". I submit that when God is taken away from the center of Christian activity and Christian service, it is no longer Christians performing the work but humanoids.

A. W. Tozer used to say that we were like the New Testament Christians only in creed. From the apostolic standpoint we were vastly different. How can we have power when we are relying on human merit rather than God's Spirit? In short, humanism has taken over and few notice or care.

We all want to be happy. Healthy. Wealthy. Successful. Was

this the standard set forth after the day of Pentecost? Did Peter tell the assembled crowd to get their finances together so they could enjoy their retirement? Did he tell them to exercise every day and work on their abs? Did he give these new converts booklets on how to have a successful ministry? Did he conduct stress relief seminars? Come on! When are we going to wake up? To be a Christian in those days meant certain imprisonment and death. If you were caught being a Christian it meant you said goodbye to your family members and waited for execution. The Church has always thrived during times of persecution. Perhaps the reason it is dying today is because it and its members are pampered rather than persecuted. I am speaking of America and Great Britain. The Church is thriving in China, Russia, India, Africa, and other nations who are paying the price for their faith. We should be crying with the prophet Isaiah, *"Woe is me"*, because we are undone by the holiness of God and the failure of His Church to live the standard He set forth in His written Word. The only woes we have are when the line in Starbucks is too long or the health spa lost one of our payments. We are a pampered, pathetic, pitiful example to a dying world. We don't care about them. We care too much about ourselves.

In this chapter we have seen how to forfeit the anointing. We will now look at how to receive the anointing.

*The Church still has a theology of the Holy
Ghost but it has no living consciousness of
His presence and power.*

—Samuel Chadwick

*It seems clear from the Scripture that it is still
the duty and privilege of believers to receive
the Holy Spirit by a conscious, definite act
of appropriating faith, just as they received
Jesus Christ.*

—A. J. Gordon

*To Thee, dear Holy Spirit,
I bring my worship now,
With reverent adoration
In prayer to Thee I bow:
As truly as I worship
The Father and the Son,
I worship thee, blest Spirit,
For Thou with Them art one.*

—J. Sidlow Baxter

*Christ must be preached in the power
of a Christ-centered, Christ-possessed,
Christ-empowered life. Christ is never
truly preached until the one who bears
the message is himself so hidden away
with Him in God that it is no longer the
messenger who speaks but Christ speaking
through him.*

—F. J. Huegel

Chapter Eighteen
THE GHOST WHO IS IGNORED

"And, being assembled together with them, commanded them that they should not depart from Jerusalem, but wait for the promise of the Father, which, saith he, ye have heard of me. For John truly baptized with water; but ye shall be baptized with the Holy Ghost not many days hence" (Acts 1:4-5).

Why are we afraid of the Holy Ghost today in evangelical circles? Why do we deny Him? Why do we not preach Him? Why do we not seek Him? Are we really afraid of ghosts—this One in particular? Jesus Christ sent us the Comforter to guide us and anoint us as believers. He is in the world to convict of sin, to draw sinners to Him. Believe it or not, the best preachers in history have been the ones with the anointing of the Holy Spirit upon their ministry. Don't fool yourself into believing the best preachers are the ones who are the most educated and have the best training—God often has the hardest time with this bunch of egotists.

Until we seek the Holy Ghost to fill us and anoint us to perform His work we are no more effective than a speaker at an insurance convention. Oh, we will stir some activity, make some noise, attain some notice from our peers, but we will lack the most important thing in our ministry: eternal fruit—the salvation of souls and the building up of the Body of Christ. We do not have to speak in tongues to have the anointing of the Holy Spirit. Is that what we are really afraid of? Come on, we

are all grown ups! Did the Holiness movement scare us away?
What was it? Whatever the reason you lack the anointing of the
Holy Ghost upon you and your ministry, you can be healed of
this disbelief in Him.

Let me state emphatically that you can forget about the Spirit
anointed ministry if you are not a holy person of God. God will
not tolerate unholiness in His messengers. If you are presently
living a double life, leave it or you will be found out and your
ministry will be in shambles. God is looking for holy men and
holy women to use for His purpose and to bring Him glory.
Speaking of glory, another thing which will keep you from "the
anointing" is a prideful desire to share in His glory. He will
have none of that!

Allow me to quote our old friend Samuel Chadwick once more,

> The Church is helpless without the presence
> and power of the Spirit .... The Church is failing to
> meet modern needs, to grip the modern mind, and
> to save modern life. The saints are the ordained
> rulers of the earth, but they do not rule; indeed,
> they have dropped the scepter and repudiated the
> responsibility. The helplessness of the Church is
> pathetic and tragic. There might be no such Person
> as the Holy Ghost.
>
> ... The Church has lost the note of authority,
> the secret of wisdom, and the gift of power through
> its persistent and wilful neglect of the Holy Spirit
> of God. Confusion and impotence are inevitable
> when the wisdom and resources of the world are
> substituted for the presence and power of the
> Spirit of God.

You see, activity has replaced authority. This is why our
young people are unimpressed with our worship services. Rather

than giving them spiritual authority that would grip their hearts we give them man-made, cookie-cutter produced activity that busies them for the moment then leaves them when they leave the building. God's authority is exciting! Man's authority is boring.

People are dulled with today's preaching. The unanointed preacher has to rely on his personality more than God's power. He has to be funny to get the audience laughing so they won't notice his lack of heavenly power. Oh, he can be interesting with his power-point message and histrionics, but he will not be effective. Almost anyone can get up in front of a group of people and lecture on some topic of interest; few can preach an on-fire message given to them by the Holy Spirit of God. What changes individual lives is not the persuasive message of a man (you can have them follow you as Stalin and Hitler proved) but the powerful Word of God which cuts to the marrow of the heart with its two edged blade. People's hearts are cold like stone to spiritual things. Only the Word of God with the illumination of the Spirit of God can break through and be a hammer which breaks the rock into pieces and turns the stoney heart into a heart of flesh.

Perhaps we lack an understanding as to who the Holy Spirit really is. Please do not be offended. I am not insinuating a lack of Biblical doctrine or theology on your part, but a lack of understanding of that knowledge. If we continue to rely upon our own strength and worldly wisdom we will grieve the Spirit away from our churches and we will be losers, for we will strive without His Presence. We will do works that are not wrought by Him. We will fail eternally in our objective to redeem the lost, to build the church, and to advance His Kingdom. We sing a hymn, "Jesus be Jesus in me". This should give us a clue to the activity and identity of the Holy Spirit.

Again we go to Chadwick,

> Jesus called the Holy Spirit the *Paraclete*.
> It is unfortunate that *"Paraclete"* should have
> been translated "Comforter," for the ministry of
> consolation hardly enters into Christ's promise.
> The margin of the Revised Version suggests the
> Latin word "Advocate" as the nearest equivalent
> to *Paraclete*, and if "Advocate" is substituted for
> "Comforter" in John 14 to 16 it is astonishing
> how illuminating it becomes. The Spirit is not
> our Advocate, but Christ's. An advocate appears
> as representative of another, and the Holy Spirit
> comes to represent Christ, to interpret and vindicate
> Christ, to administer for Christ in His Church and
> Kingdom. He comes to be to the believer all that
> Christ Himself was and is—with this difference:
> that Christ was with His disciples and the Spirit
> is in them.

The Apostle Paul stated, "Christ liveth in me". Through this
understanding we can say the same!

Believers today have the attitude "Relax and be raptured".

—Leonard Ravenhill

When Self vacates the throne, and Christ becomes the center of our personality, then everything is adjusted to His sovereign will.

—John Gregory Mantle

I am only an ordinary man. I have no special gifts. I am no orator, no scholar, no profound thinker. If I have done anything for Christ and my generation, it is because I have given myself entirely to Christ Jesus, and then tried to do whatever He wanted me to do.

—F. B. Meyer

And the Holy Ghost descended in a bodily shape like a dove upon him, and a voice came from heaven, which said, Thou art my beloved Son; in thee I am well pleased.

—Luke 3:22

Chapter Nineteen

BY MY SPIRIT

"Not by might, nor by power, but by My Spirit saith the LORD of hosts" (Zech. 4:6).

Now that we have a better understanding of who the Holy Spirit is and how He administers the activity of Christ through the people of God, let us look at how He empowers his people to perform His work. Our text in Zechariah is profound. After the Babylonian captivity, Joshua and Zerubbabel were busy in their work of restoring the temple. They needed help. It was Zechariah's task to inform dutiful Zerubbabel that the work of restoring the temple and the nation of Judah would be better accomplished if they did not rely upon the might and power of man but upon the Spirit of the Lord of hosts. It is a hard lesson for each of us to learn as we build our temples and work our fleshly might.

With the Holy Spirit anointing us we can do the work of God. Without the Holy Spirit anointing us we can do the work of man. What we have predominately in our churches today is the work of man and it smells of man—the stink of decay. On a recent visit to a funeral home, I had to walk the corridors to arrive at the back office to pick up a death certificate. As I walked through the silence of the building, I observed an occasional corpse laid out for viewing that day. And as I walked, very quickly I might add, the Spirit of God spoke to my heart. In the still and quiet of that building which contained the vestige of death, the still Spirit of the Lord said, "Look around you. Do you see the deadness here? The coldness and lack of life? This is My Church today—lifeless and without activity".

Well, I could have argued with the Voice that He was wrong for there is much activity within the churches today. But He is never wrong—we are. The activity He was referring to was His activity. There is little activity in His name and administered by Him because we refuse to allow Him to do His work—we would rather exclude Him entirely and build our own temples in our name for our own glory; not His. Just as He called the decaying Lazurus from the cold dark tomb, He is calling us today to "come alive" if we will only hear His voice. But through the noise of the pounding of the nails and hammers of our own efforts we block out the only helping Hand which can truly help. We neglect and reject the only power which can truly save. We ignore and affront a Holy God who is standing outside the Church knocking, asking to come in and we say, "No one is home; go away". And in many of our churches today He has gone away and the sad pitiful thing of it all is this: like Samson, we are oblivious to the Spirit of God having left us. We find out when we, like Samson, are confronted with the enemy and the enemy is too overpowering for us to have victory in our own strength. Then, and only then, do we cry out to God for help; but by then the hole we have dug for ourselves is as deep as the one Joseph was cast into and we cannot get out.

It may be that we overbuilt our ministry with too many buildings and now the debt cannot be carried. Or perhaps we hired staff members which we now regret and cannot remove because we did not seek His counsel to begin with. Or perhaps we undertook a mission project too big for man but not too big for God, but by our efforts and our flesh we are struggling in failure. And as we fail, we finally realize that we weren't that smart or powerful after all; we are merely humans attempting to do supernatural work without supernatural help. When will we learn?! Now. Now we can learn.

If you are at this point in your ministry where the only way to turn is up, then look to Him for help and He will never fail you nor forsake you. If you are not at this juncture in ministry and all is still well with your soul, stop and evaluate your purposes. Are you purpose driven or God led?

In the next chapter we will examine how to seek a better understanding of the person and work of the Holy Spirit.

God is His own interpreter and He will make it plain.

—William Cowper

Stephen's day of ministry had scarcely begun when it was violently ended, but the greatness of one's life must not be looked for in length of days. Stephen means "crown", and early did he receive his.

—W. Graham Scroggie

Holy Spirit, reign in me,
With your own authority—
That my life, with constancy,
May "flesh out" your liberty.

—Stephen F. Olford

The only man with whom Jesus Christ will speak is the man of a broken heart; a broken and a contrite spirit He will not despise.

—Joseph Parker

Chapter Twenty

HIS OWN INTERPRETER

"For the prophecy came not in old time by the will of man: but holy men of God spake as they were moved by the Holy Ghost" (2 Pet. 1:21).

Spiritual work is significant work; it is the only work worth living and dying for. What a tragedy it would be to appear at the Judgement Seat of Christ believing our ministry and life here on this earth had been a tremendous success only to find out it was wood, hay, and stubble. The flames of eternal judgement will burn our life work before our tear stained eyes. Sadly, this will be the case for many. Let it not be the case for you. Knowledge is empowerment and the Holy Spirit can give you both knowledge and power to do His work for His plan and purpose—not ours.

The Apostle Paul had much to say regarding the Holy Spirit and His work. For him it was all the difference between the man he was in Romans chapter seven and the man he became in Romans chapter eight. In Romans chapter eight Paul makes mention of the Holy Spirit nineteen times. He speaks of mortifying the deeds of the body and tells us to walk not after the flesh but after the Spirit. He tells us that those who are in the flesh cannot please God and he makes the bold statement that, *"Now if any man have not the Spirit of Christ he is none of his." Romans 8:9.* Paul instructs us in 2 Corinthians, *"Now the Lord is that Spirit: and where the Spirit of the Lord is, there is liberty" (3:17).* And in Galatians he tells us, *"If we live in the Spirit, let us also walk in the Spirit" (5:25).*

So Paul is telling us that to be Christians we have to have the Spirit, to have liberty we have to have the Spirit, and then he tells us to walk in the Spirit. Let me pose a question: when Paul speaks about not being weary in well doing (Gal. 6:9) is he performing his well-doing void of the Spirit? Of course not! If this was good enough for the Apostle Paul why is it so hard for us? Do you believe that this spiritual giant of a man (though only a man) would have dared to storm the gates of hell in all those decadent cities in Greece proclaiming the gospel without the Spirit of God upon him? If he had, we probably never would have heard of him. He would have made a noise for a little while like we do and that would have been it. But rather this God-sent man tells us plainly that his Christian character is not developed by self effort and physical strength but produced by the Holy Spirit alone; and the fruit of this life is, *"love, joy, peace, longsuffering, gentleness, goodness, faith, meekness, temperance" (Gal. 5:22).* In his majestic epistle to the Ephesians, he warns us not to grieve the Spirit and then he orders believers to be filled with the Spirit; Ephesians 4:30-5:18. He then reveals the way to prayer by conquering our foe, *"Praying always with all prayer and supplication in the Spirit" (Eph. 6:18).*

What are we doing in our lives and ministries that keeps us from this biblical model of power? One of the classics on the work of the Holy Spirit is the book by Handley G. G. Moule, *Veni Creator*. In it he states,

> But are we filled, nay are we filling, with the Spirit? Is His blessed power upon our "first springs of thought and will" a power fully welcomed there? Are we watching and praying over the matter, and humbly resolved, looking up for light, that nothing we know of in act, or habit, in occupation, in recreation, in thought and word about our neighbor, in use of time or means, is

such as to obstruct the rise of His "calm excess"
through all we are and all we have? ... we are to
be filled, and to be full of Him, as those who have
already received Him "from the height that knows
no measure."

It is time for us to reexamine this important doctrine of the
Holy Spirit and to apply it to our lives. When we by faith seek
this blessing it will alter our ministries as nothing else can—
supernaturally.

This supernatural walk will empower your ministry beyond
measure. Rather than going through your busy schedule each
week relying on your talents and self-effort, you will find you
can do more in less time and achieve greatness without striving
to be great. At the funeral service of A. W. Tozer, there was
an old saint who knew him well. This man prayed an old-
time prayer using Thee and Thou, wouldst and couldst. You
could tell by listening to him he knew the Lord well. Then this
man mentioned the life of Dr. Tozer in this regard: "Oh God,
it is truly amazing what you can do with a competent and
consecrated man". Do you realize how much is said in those
two adjectives? Competent and consecrated. Think about
that. God is not looking for brilliant men—though he certainly
uses them. God is not looking for handsome men—though he
certainly uses them. He is looking for men who are two things:
competent and consecrated. The definition of competent is
"adequate for the purpose". The definition of consecrated is
"set apart for holy use". Did you get that?

God is looking for individuals who are adequate for His
purpose and set apart for Him. That is all. Why do we make
being a Christian so hard? He wants us to be obedient and
available. He will do the rest. Once we get to the place in our
Christian walk where we are "set apart", as Aaron and the tribe
of Levi were set apart for the service of God, then God will in

the words of Cowper, "do wonders to perform".

Listen to another "Christian Classic". This one is by Major Ian Thomas:

> If you will but trust Christ, not only for the death He died in order to redeem you, but also for the life that He lives and waits to live through you, the very next step you take will be a step taken in the very energy and power of God Himself. You will have begun to live a life which is essentially supernatural, yet still clothed with the common humanity of your physical body, and still worked out in the things that inevitably make up the lot of a man who, though his heart may be with Christ in heaven, still has his two feet firmly planted on the earth.

*Quite suddenly, upon one and another came
an overwhelming sense of the reality and
awfulness of His presence and of eternal things.*
—Joseph Kemp

*The awful presence of God brought a
wave of conviction of sin that caused even
mature Christians to feel their sinfulness,
bringing groans of distress and prayers of
repentance from the unconverted. Strong
men were bowed under the weight of sin
and cries for mercy were mingled with
shouts of joy from others who had passed
into life.*
—Duncan Campbell

*Faithful, and often owned of God,
Vessel of grace, by Jesus used;
Stir up the gift on thee bestowed,
The gift by hallowed hands transfused.*
—Charles Wesley

*I share the view of E. M. Bounds that it
takes God twenty years to make a preacher.*
—Leonard Ravenhill

Chapter Twenty-One
VESSEL BEARING

"Be ye clean, that bear the vessels of the Lord" (Isa. 52:11).

This chapter is on holiness. Not the holiness of God, but our holiness unto God. The awesome responsibility upon us to *"bear the vessels of the Lord"* is a task most of us are not up to without help from above. That help comes in the form of the Holy Spirit. He is the enabler to accomplish divine tasks. If we miss it here, we miss it everywhere! Pay attention. Sit up straight. God's work is to be done. The howls at the Bema Seat will be many as we realize how far we fell short of this objective; holiness. Christians understood this better two or three generations ago. I'm afraid the times in which we live (television, internet, and moral decay all about us) have saturated our lives with sinful images and it is tougher to be holy today than say, in Bible times. However, though the demands of God's mandates are heavier in modern times, they nonetheless are more vital in this hour than ever before!

If you are a minister reading this and you are not practicing holiness—shame on you! Your laziness here, your selfishness here, will bite you some day. You will be found out, for Scripture states there is nothing hidden that will not be made known. We are commanded to be holy. If we fail here—we fail everywhere. You will never have power from on High if you lack holiness. Forget it. Plan out a man-centered format for your ministry (there are numerous best-sellers to help you do this) and be off on your fleshly way. Good luck. You will need luck since you will be traveling without God. Strong words. Yes, but strong words are needful in these dreadful days of moral downgrade in the pulpit. Don't play games with God, mister. For the game you are playing is Devil's solitaire. There have been men and women of faith in history whose lives stand out in holiness: Amy Carmichael, Corrie Ten Boom, Robert Murray M'Cheyne, John Wesley, Frances Havergal, Fanny Crosby, George Whitefield, F. B. Meyer, and David Brainard to name only a few. These sanctified men and women were used of God greatly. Why? They were consecrated individuals who cared more about heaven than about earth. Each breath they took was in the light of eternity. What about you? Can it be said of you that you are a holy man or holy woman of God? Please do not confuse holiness with legalism! Are you seeking holiness? Or are you just a professional Christian? The world already has too many professional Christians and not enough holy ones. Which rank do you fall in? Please do not confuse holiness with being busily occupied with Christian service. Let me ask you this question plainly, DOES GOD CONSIDER YOU A HOLY SERVANT OF HIS?

What can you do about it? Plenty! The first item on your agenda is death. Yes, death. You must be willing to die to the self life. If you do not fully comprehend Galatians 2:20 I suggest you go out and buy a copy of *Not I But Christ* by Dr. Stephen F. Olford or buy a copy of *Born Crucified* by L. E. Maxwell. Let me quote from these two men who understood this concept better than their peers.

Regarding the Christ-life for the self-life, Stephen Olford writes:

Years in the ministry have taught me that many people endure the Christian life rather than enjoy it. They know what it is to be forgiven for their sins. They have the hope of heaven. But in between that initial experience of saving faith and that final experience of seeing Jesus there is a vast gap characterized by barrenness, frustration, and failure.

The fact is, only one person ever lived the Christian life; it was Jesus ... after effecting that eternal salvation through the blood of His cross and the power of His resurrection, He ascended to heaven to impart His life, through the Holy Spirit, to all who believe His gospel and receive His full salvation. So the Christian life is nothing less than "the outliving of the indwelling Christ" on the principle of dependent faith. The Apostle Paul sums it up in the words that are the theme and thrust of this book: *"I have been crucified with Christ; it is no longer I who live, but Christ lives in me; and the life which I now live in the flesh I live by faith in the Son of God, who loved me and gave Himself for me" (Gal. 2:20).*

"The miracle of the indwelling life of Christ is made possible by the power of the Holy Spirit.

Anyone who knows my mentor Stephen Olford knows he is one thing (besides being a great preacher); he is a holy man of God. He helped Billy Graham find the anointing in Wales when Billy Graham was just a young lanky lad. Billy Graham has unction. And so can you! God may not use you like he used a Billy Graham, but He has use for you nonetheless! Are you willing to "give it all to Him"?

Choices we make often determine our course in life. Are we living for self or Christ? I did not ask you if you were in the ministry. Who are you living for? What are you living for? Allow me to quote a classic on the crucified life, *Born Crucified;*

My friend, the Lord is coming. What is your life? Is it lived in the Spirit? Oh the power of the Cross to sever every relationship that would bind us to the flesh! We are debtors only to the Holy Spirit. Give the Cross full place in your life; abandon yourself recklessly to the Crucified, for over His crucified life the flesh has not one speck of power. Let the Cross seize upon you and sever you from that dominating thralldom to the flesh. "Every strong conviction ends by taking possession of us; it overcomes and absorbs us, and tears us ruthlessly from everything else." Has the Cross so seized upon your life? If it has, you can live for self nevermore. Rather, you will cry out with a determined saint of yore, "Oh my God, hear the cries of one on whom Thou hast had mercy, and prepare my heart to receive whatever Christ has purchased for me. Allow me not to rest short of it. Put a thorn in every enjoyment, a worm in every gourd, that would either prevent my being wholly thine, or in any measure retard my progress in the divine life" (T. C. Upham).

We should be separated from the world in all we do. We should not blend in and act like they would. We will look at this idea further in the next chapter on separation.

Worldliness only flourishes when the vitality of the church is low and, as the church is composed of units, when the vitality of the individual is low.

—John Gregory Mantle

Worldliness is human activity with God left out. Worldliness is life without heavenly callings, life without ideals, life without heights. Worldliness recognizes nothing of the high calling of God in Christ Jesus: Worldliness has not hill country. Worldliness is a horizontal life. Worldliness has nothing of the vertical in it. It has ambition; it has no aspirations. Its motto is success, not holiness. It is always saying, "Onward", never "Upward".

—Dr. J. H. Jowett

But God forbid that I should glory, save in the cross of our Lord Jesus Christ, by whom the world is crucified unto me, and I unto the world.

—Galatians 6:14

Heaven begins in the "heart", down here, before it is consumated in the "home", up there.

—J. Sidlow Baxter

Chapter Twenty-Two

CHRISTIAN SEPARATION

"If any man will come after me, let him deny himself, and take up his cross, and follow me. For whosoever will save his life shall lose it: and whosoever will lose his life for my sake shall find it" (Matt. 16:24-25).

Jesus was separate from the world in all He did during His earthly ministry. Though He walked through villages intermingling with humanity He remained separate from the world. The Apostle Peter reminds us we are to be a peculiar people walking as strangers and pilgrims in this world.

Christian separation is a topic seldom discussed from pulpits today. J. Sidlow Baxter used to comment that if a visiting preacher wished to be disinvited from returning to a church, then he should preach Christian separation from the world. No one wants to hear it. It is a message without an audience. It cost W. Graham Scroggie his first two pastorates. It kicked Leonard Ravenhill out from many a pulpit. We have to ask ourselves this, do we wish to be popular or obedient to the Bible? The Apostle Paul never sought popularity.

What is Christian separation? Do we even know? It is nonconformity to the world: its fashions, its attainments, its standards, its goals, its driving desires, and much more. Peter told us what believers are in God's eyes, *"But ye are a chosen generation, a royal priesthood, an holy nation, a peculiar people; that ye should shew forth the praises of him who hath called you out of darkness into his marvellous light: which in time past were not a people, but are now the people of God: which had not obtained mercy, but now have obtained mercy" (1 Pet. 2:9-10).*

Do we dare preach Christian separation from our pulpits? Do we dare not? Do we dare not to live it in example to a perishing world around us? Few understood this better than the Apostle Paul, *"But God forbid that I should glory, save in the cross of our Lord Jesus Christ, by whom the world is crucified unto me, and I unto the world" (Gal. 6:14).* As this defender of the faith walked the streets of Ephesus he could see all the world had to offer. Across the street from the magnificent library of Celsus was the city brothel. The revenues from the brothel helped support the city of Ephesus. This ancient city was a center of religious activity, for the Ephesians worshiped the goddess Diana and the great temple there was one of the seven wonders of the world. Also the theater at Ephesus (carved out of the side of a mountain) played host to the best entertainment in the province of Asia. Because of the city's major trade routes, Ephesus was prosperous and it offered all the attractions of the world to its half million inhabitants. It had all the allurements of a pagan society geared toward satisfying the desires of the flesh yet Paul could say, *"And be not conformed to this world: but be ye transformed by the renewing of your mind, that ye may prove what is that good, and acceptable, and perfect, will of God" (Rom. 12:2).*

God called His people Israel to be a separate nation from the Gentiles surrounding them. Today He calls Christians to be a separate people in the pagan world in which we live. In his diary, David Brainerd recorded his daily nonconformity to the world. A missionary to the Indians around New York in the mid seventeen hundreds, Brainerd died daily to the world and its amusements, "Life itself now appeared but an empty bubble; the riches, honors, and common enjoyments of life appeared extremely tasteless. I longed to be perpetually and entirely crucified to all things here below, by the cross of Christ … it was my meat and drink to be holy, to live to the Lord, and die to the Lord".

Brainerd, who died in the service of our Lord in his twenty ninth year, knew the emptiness of the world and its amusements.

CHRISTIAN SEPARATION

Educated at Yale, David Brainerd was a close friend to Jonathan Edwards. And Jonathan Edwards also knew Christian separation for he himself was the author of 70 resolutions which he reviewed on a weekly basis to be sure he was continually crucified to the world as well. Some of his resolutions were, "Resolved, That I will live so, as I shall wish I had done when I come to die ... Resolved, when I feel pain, to think of the pains of martyrdom and hell ... Resolved, Never to do any manner of thing, whether in soul or body, less or more, but what tends to the glory of God".

God used each of these men in mighty ways. Edwards was used in the mighty revival of The Great Awakening which spread through Northampton in New England and Brainerd was an example of godliness in a consecrated man dead to the world. His life has influenced thousands including the saintly Robert Murray M'Cheyne who cried out early in life, "O for Brainerd's humility and sin-loathing dispositions!" M'Cheyne himself died at the tender age of twenty-nine—his life completely spent from serving his Lord. It was said of Robert Murray M'Cheyne that he could enter a room and silence it with his emanating holiness. M'Cheyne wrote, "I am persuaded that I shall obtain the highest amount of present happiness, I shall do most for God's glory and the good of man, and I shall have the fullest reward in eternity, by maintaining a conscience always washed in Christ's blood, by being filled with the Holy Spirit at all times, and by attaining the most entire likeness to Christ in mind, will, and heart, that is possible for a redeemed sinner to attain in this world".

It is imperative for each of us to attain to heavenly things while here on earth; our minds should be stayed there, our bodies should be consecrated to there, our lives should be consumed with the priorities of heaven, our hearts should be focused on heavenly things, and our time here as strangers should be spent in the service of our King who resides there at the right hand of the Father.

If we only spent more of our time in looking at Him we should soon forget ourselves.
                              —Martyn Lloyd-Jones

I give Thee my body: may I glorify Thee with it, and preserve it holy, fit for Thee, O God, to dwell in. May I neither indulge it, nor use too much rigor towards it; but keep it, as far as in me lies, healthy, vigorous, and active, and fit to do Thee all manner of service which Thou shalt call for.
                              —John Wesley

Jesus said unto him, If thou wilt be perfect, go and sell that thou hast, and give to the poor, and thou shalt have treasure in heaven: and come and follow me.
                              —Matthew 19:21

"So Joseph died being an hundred and ten years old: and they embalmed him, and he was put in a coffin in Egypt". Thus ends Genesis. It begins with creation and ends with a coffin. It begins with the glory and ends with a grave. It begins with the vastness of eternity and ends with the shortness of time.
                              —John Phillips

Chapter Twenty-Three
OUR STEWARDSHIP

"And he called him, and said unto him, How is it that I hear this of thee? Give an account of thy stewardship; for thou mayest be no longer steward" (Luke 16:2).

Jesus had much to say on the stewardship of His followers. He spoke of the kingdom of heaven *"Likened unto a certain king , which would take account of his servants" (Matt. 18:23).* Our Lord spoke of the man traveling into a far country who called his servants and delivered unto them all his goods. He had deep things to say of their stewardship of the talents he left them. There were rewards for those who handled them well and harsh words for those who did not. *"Thou wicked and slothful servant ... Take therefore the talent from him ... cast ye the unprofitable servant into outer darkness: there shall be weeping and gnashing of teeth" (Matt. 25:26, 28, 30).*

Our stewardship of heavenly things while we are in our earthly body will determine much we cannot now see. But it will be revealed to us on that day. We have little idea now the imperativeness and the graveness of this matter of stewardship. A. W. Tozer used to say that he was not so much worried about how he lived his life for Christ (regarding the judgment seat for believers) but of the things he had not done for Him. The solemnity of that comment by Tozer should raise the hairs on the back of our spiritual necks. Have we ever examined this aspect of the Christian life as it relates to our personal lives and ministry for Him?

Let us look at this matter of stewardship more closely. The

Greek word *epitropos* means "someone who is a manager". The Greek word *oikonomos* means "one who is an overseer". These terms mean "one who managed one's affairs or was a superintendent of one's household". In Unger's Bible Dictionary it is stated, "We read of Joseph's steward and of Herod's steward ... as great confidence was reposed in these officials. Paul describes Christian ministers as the stewards of God over His church (1 Cor. 4:1-2 *'those given a trust,'* NIV). Believers are also said to be stewards of God, of God's gifts and graces (1 Pet. 4:10).

In the Old Testament in the book of Isaiah we read, *"Wherefore do ye spend money for that which is not bread?" (Isa. 55:2)*. And in the book of Ecclesiastes we find, *"Cast thy bread upon the waters: for thou shalt find it after many days" (11:1)*. These verses are in reference to the stewardship of our finances. In the book of Proverbs we read, *"The slothful man saith, There is a lion without, I shall be slain in the streets" (Prov. 22:13)*. The Apostle Paul instructs us, *"See then, that ye walk circumspectly, not as fools, but as wise. Redeeming the time, because the days are evil". (Eph. 5:15-16)*. These verses speak of how we spend our time; industriously or lazily, foolishly or wisely. Paul mentions that we are to be good stewards with our bodies, *"I beseech you therefore, brethren, by the mercies of God, that ye present your bodies a living sacrifice, holy, acceptable unto God, which is your reasonable service" (Rom. 12:1)*.

Let us now examine the various ways in which stewardship applies to the Christian. We will list them accordingly:

We are to be good stewards of:
- OUR TIME
- OUR MONEY
- OUR BODIES
- OUR TALENTS OR GIFTS

We will look at these one at a time. First let us examine how we spend **OUR TIME.** As Christians we need to tread very carefully here, for this is a category we seldom think about. How we actually spend our time and how Jesus Christ desires us to spend our time are two entirely different matters. We tend to view our lives from OUR CENTER pertaining to OUR ACTIVITIES and relating to OUR PERSONAL AGENDA. He, on the other hand, desires His disciples and followers to spend their time WITH HIM AS THE CENTER focusing the attention of all of OUR ACTIVITIES on Him and relating them to HIS HEAVENLY AGENDA for His supreme purpose to bring Him glory and to bring good to man. What we do with the twenty-four hours which He allots us each day is crucial to our service to Him. We can either be productive for heaven or wasteful on earth. We briefly covered this topic in the questionnaire in chapter sixteen. We will spend time wisely here delving deeper into this critical matter.

Please take the time to prayerfully do the following:

1. I will each day write in a journal how much time I spent with God in prayer.
   I will each day write in a journal how much time I spent in recreational activities.
2. I will each day record in my daily journal the following:

   • time spent watching televison or movies;
   • time spent surfing the internet;
   • time spent performing a favorite sport or hobby;
   • time spent in wasteful and time consuming conversation with friends or co-workers.

4. How much time did I spend in Bible study and reading holy Scripture?
5. How much time did I waste in selfish activities?

6.   How much time did I use wisely for God?

We will now cover the topic of **OUR MONEY.** This will be one of the hardest things you will ever do because we are conditioned to think as the world here. Contrary to the system of the world, we are not to lay up treasures in retirement plans and assets. Working toward a retirement of ease where we play golf every day, or fish, or hunt, or travel, or whatever is the WORLD'S SYSTEM not ours! We are not to drive luxury automobiles to impress our friends and satisfy our overblown egos. Now I am losing some readers at this point because this is coming too close to home. The point I am making is not legalism but changing the way we think about these things. I spent a fortune over the years on foreign and luxury cars. Why? Shallowness on my part. Then God finally awakened me to this grievous error of wasting His money. I began to view how I spent money in light of eternity. That is what changed everything. I now will skip eating lunch at a favorite restaurant and take the money I would have spent on that lunch (I either brown bag my lunch or go home) and give it to foreign missions. I do this with things such as washing my car (I used to spend a great deal of money each week having my car washed). I now do it myself and give that money to missions. See the point? These are merely examples and ways to reorient our focus from US to OTHERS. Have you bought into the world's concept of wealth accumulation? It is okay to make money and invest it wisely but for what purpose? Are you planning on leaving it all to your spouse and children? Making your children rich when you die is probably one of the worst things you can do to them. Few can handle instant prosperity. Do you get my point? Pray that the Lord will change our focus on money and its use while we are stewards of it here on earth. The one with the most toys at the end of life is a loser—not a winner.

The next unpopular topic (especially for ministers) is **OUR**

BODY. Let's see why.

Yes, Paul said that bodily exercise profitith little. But that does not mean we are to not be prudent with how we treat our bodies. John Wesley ate little and saved little. When he died an old man he was trim in body and in his physical possessions were six silver spoons. He lived his life in light of eternity. So should we. We should have temperance in eating and drinking. We should exercise on a regular basis. A complaint I often hear of preachers from the unsaved is that they are too overweight.

Let me relate a story by the late L. E. Maxwell, founder of the Prairie Bible Institute.

A personal friend of the writer passed away a few years ago. This lady had been brought up to believe that what she liked her system needed and must have—whether food or raiment. She was not extravagant. Her life just centered in her likes and tastes and preferences. To these she daily bowed. She liked color, bright red especially. She liked fats, was very fond of sweets. She clung to these things "as a cat clings to its home". They were her life. But the Saviour said, "He that loveth his life shall lose it". That is more than theology. It is a great fact, a principle of life; it is inexorable law. And it obtains even in this world. The very things we love are the very things we lose; find them distasteful to us, and that sooner than we think. Some months before passing away, color became unbearable to this lady. The flesh had to have bright red covered up. Her whole being revolted at fats. As to sweets—well, the least sugar became sickening. These had been her life—now she loathed them. She had loved her life, had never lost it, refused to lose it—now she loathed it.

Brethren I need not say more on losing weight, eating properly, and exercise—the world is watching us and we have great tasks before us; let us take better care of the vessel before she sinks!

The next topic for review is **OUR TALENTS OR GIFTS.** We all have some talent or gift in a particular area. Some are multi-talented and multi-gifted. How do we use these God-given gifts and talents? Do we use them for our own gratification, seeking applause and compliments of others? Do we sing or play an instrument merely to be heard and applauded on our ability? Do we preach because we like the sound of our voice? Do we serve for a pat on the back and recognition? What is the motive behind our service? We will be judged at the Bema Seat for what we have done in the body and the motives behind what we have done in the service of our King.

Do we share in His glory? Do we delight when the crowd has come to hear US? Are we offended when the one introducing us forgets one of our accolades? Do we desire the best seat in the room? Do we even pay attention to these things which are recorded daily in a book. The book of life. There is a book being written about us daily. It is our biography in God's eyes. From our birth to our death there is a record of all we have thought, said, and done while in the body here upon earth. On a future day the books will be opened and there will be a cosmic review of our lives. I say cosmic because it will be alien to how we view things here and now. The importance of the world will be absent; the opinion of our peers and friends will be absent; all of the ego and all that which is of the flesh will be absent when the One with eyes of flame will reward us for the things done in the body. He will try our works, *"For other foundation can no man lay than that is laid, which is Jesus Christ. Now if any man build upon this foundation gold, silver, precious stones, wood, hay, stubble; Every man's work shall be made manifest: for the day shall declare it, because it shall be revealed by fire; and the fire shall try every man's work of what sort it is. If any man's work abide which he hath built thereupon, he shall receive a reward. If any man's work shall be burned, he shall suffer loss: but he himself shall be saved; yet so as by fire" (1 Cor. 3:11-15).*

What kind of rewards shall you have? Charred stubble or gleaming gems?

"I'm living off the dividends of a well spent life."
—*R. G. Lee*

When we are nearing the end of the way and life's sun is sinking low, if on looking back we can see nothing but a life spent in the service of God, walking in the light of His Word, this will afford us untold satisfaction.
—*Charles E. Orr*

Only one life 'twill soon be past, only what's done for Christ will last; and as I lay dying how good it shall be if the lamp of my life has been burned out for Thee.
—*C. T. Studd*

The Apostle Paul, Luther, Wesley, Whitefield, Knox, Edwards, Finney, Spurgeon, Moody, each shared a common denominator; a fire in their belly. They each were so eaten up with the Gospel and thirsty for Christ and filled with the Holy Ghost—they could not stand idly by while others perished. They saw nothing but eternity, worshiped a Holy God, and served a Risen Christ; living not for earth nor its gains but living only for heaven and its rewards. When they preached they linked the Devil with sin and the Cross with salvation. They preached hell and its fire and Christ and Him crucified. Not one of them feared King, Queen, or Pope; and not one of them sought the compliments of men.
—*E. A. Johnston*

Chapter Twenty-Four
HIS PURPOSE AND GREAT DESIGN

"And we know that all things work together for good to them that love God, to them who are the called according to his purpose" (Rom. 8:28).

We each have a design purpose for our lives if we are called by His Name and sealed by His Spirit. It is this: to bring Him glory while we are here upon earth, and to do the will of Him who saved us. Are we effective in this mighty calling and task? Are we fulfilling and meeting this divine objective? Are we aligned properly to His purpose and great design? Or are we aligned selfishly to our purpose and our designs? Do some soul searching here and ask the Holy Spirit to realign us to His agenda. Here are some steps which can help us; we must ask ourselves:

- AM I IN ACCORD WITH HIS PLANS FOR MY LIFE?
- AM I IN THE RIGHT PROFESSION, JOB, MINISTRY?
- HAVE I SAID "NO" TO HIS CALLING ME TO A PARTICULAR AREA?
- AM I AT THE RIGHT CHURCH FROM—HIS PERSPECTIVE?
- IS MY HOME LIFE IN ORDER AND PLEASING TO HIM?
- ARE MY THOUGHTS HIS THOUGHTS?
- LIKE JOB, DO I PLACE A GUARD OVER MY EYES EACH DAY?
- AM I SEEKING HOLINESS IN ALL I SAY AND DO?

- DO I HAVE A HEART FOR THE LOST?
- DO I HAVE A HEART FOR FOREIGN MISSIONS?
- DO I WITNESS FOR HIM?
- DO I WASTE MONEY FOOLISHLY IN THE LIGHT OF ETERNITY?
- DO I WASTE TIME CARELESSLY IN THE LIGHT OF ETERNITY?
- DO I BRING HIM HONOR AND GLORY IN ALL I SAY AND DO?
- CAN OTHERS SAY OF ME THAT I AM CHRISTLIKE IN CHARACTER?

This is just a beginning. Pray the Lord to show other areas that are perhaps more germane to you and your ministry. Care about the things He cares about. Jesus said, *"where I am, there shall also my servant be"* (John 12:26). Have you sought where the Lord is working and have you followed Him there or are you off working one place while He is distinctly at another? Remember, revival comes when we get serious with Him in every area of our life; He will get serious with us when we get serious with Him.

Do you pray before you act? Or do you act and then ask God to bless those actions? Do you know you are in the center of His will or is there doubt? Do you have confirmation that you are doing the right thing and are where you need to be right now? Ask yourself this last question: "Can God say of me that I am a close friend of His and that I am a dependable servant for Him?"

Are you living for Him? Are you really living for Him? Let me quote one verse before we go to the last chapter in the book. Jesus made a remark to His disciples prior to Calvary. It was foretelling of Calvary and His work there, but the remark goes deeper than that (if it possibly can). Jesus told them, *"Verily, verily, I say unto you, except a corn of wheat fall into the ground and die, it abideth alone: but if it die, it bringeth forth much fruit"* (John 12:24). This verse meant only the obvious to me for years until the Holy Spirit made a personal application of it to my life. This was the application:

If we live to ourselves we will lack the kind of fruit which Christ deems profitable—fruit that multiplies and remains. To have this kind of fruit we must be like the corn of wheat. We too must fall into the ground and die. Let me explain. To fall means to give way to a force greater than ourselves; in this case gravity. To fall means to let go completely. When one dies they fall to the ground, for their self support system of personal energy no longer holds them up. To be the corn of wheat means to let go, to fall and let God take us from there, to die to ourselves; our desires, our goals, our passions of likes and dislikes, to die to our personality and ego; to give up all existence apart from Him the giver of life. This way, and only by this way, can God use us in the way He desires to. Then and only then will we be fruitful, not from our perspective but FROM HIS PERSPECTIVE. Do you get it? Can you do it? Pray that you can!

Let us move on to the final chapter in this book, but hopefully the beginning chapters of a new walk and ministry for HIM.

Restore unto me the joy of my salvation;
—Psalms 51:12

Joyful, joyful, we adore Thee, God of glory
Lord of love.
—Henry Van Dyke

Those who climb highest could fall farthest,
if they slipped.
—Guy H. King

Live so as to be missed.
—Robert Murray M'Cheyne

Chapter Twenty-Five

JOYFUL IN THE LORD

"And my soul shall be joyful in the Lord: it shall rejoice in his salvation" (Ps. 35:9).

When revival comes, whether personal, in the local church, or globally in the Church around the world, one thing is for certain; there will be JOY, JOY, JOY! The burden of life lifts so quickly when revival finally comes and God displays His glory. When we see Him for who He is, we worship Him in a joyful way unlike before! Our face will shine with a newness like the morning sun because we have been bathing in the light of the Everlasting Son. We will sing praises to Him with our hearts full of love for Him and it will seem at times we cannot contain our emotions for Him.

God in all His glory, God in all His Majesty, God in all His sovereignty. This state will mirror our state in eternity, forever worshipping Him and adoring Him! However, this state here does not always last. Revival comes and it goes. God manifests Himself and He leaves. Why does this happen? It is our fault, not His. We grieve Him away. In the history of revival when He has shown Himself and performed His wonders He has never stayed; humankind has always grieved Him away. He does not change; we do. If it is a local revival in a church, we begin to take credit for it. Or perhaps we begin to criticize others. Or we begin to behave in the flesh rather than Spirit. We end up doing something to grieve Him away. Perhaps He leaves for He knows our frail bodies cannot sustain the physical demands of revival. On a personal level, where we have had a newness in our walk with Him, this can continue for the rest of our lives if we continue to seek it. He will be faithful if we diligently continue to seek Him and seek His likeness.

I only mention this passing of revival because it is inevitable. There has never been a continuous revival, whether local or national. It always ends. The Christian life, as we well know, is not all mountaintop experience, but is comprised of valley experience as well. Highs and lows. Even our examples of those who went before us show us this. Elijah triumphed over 4000 prophets of Baal then sank in despair beneath a juniper tree wishing to die. Jonah saved an entire city through his witness for God then cried to die when the worm ate his gourd. We will each have our gourds, our juniper trees. The victorious Christian is the one who turns back to God and lays in His everlasting arms and admits he or she cannot do a thing apart from Him. The victorious Christian will pick himself up and go seeking after God even if God seems a million miles away. The victorious Christian will say like Paul, though sitting in chains and awaiting certain execution, *"If we suffer, we shall also reign with him: if we deny him, he also will deny us"* (2 Tim. 2:12).

Let us never fear suffering for Him and let us never deny Him, let us press on toward the mark. And we can say with Paul, *"And the Lord shall deliver me from every evil work, and will preserve me unto his heavenly kingdom: to whom be glory for ever and ever. Amen"* (2 Tim. 4:18).

Even though the Apostle Paul was in chains, deserted by many, he still had joy in the Lord. Though our circumstance may dictate our present happiness or lack of it, we may still have joy in our Lord.

AFTERWORD

Let us remember that revival begins in prayer. It is birthed through travailing prayer and a contrite heart. As we cry out to Him, whether for the nation, the Church, or for ourselves, He will answer either in a personal way or en masse. Remember the order: Prayer, Repentance, Revival.

If we know all this, why not act upon it? What is keeping you from taking your church through this revival process? Is it your reputation? Is it laziness? Are we too comfortable enjoying things the way they are in status quo to rock the boat? Do we lack faith in Him? Do we trust too much in ourselves? Perhaps we like taking credit for our activities and do not wish to share any glory with Him. God have mercy upon us! Repent. Cry out. Pray. Wake up! God visits in the darkest hour in the last watch of the night—but only if we are staying up through the night seeking Him. While we sleep the world perishes. While we snore the Evil One labors and hell fills up with cries of torment; how can we hear their cries if we slumber? What will it take before the leaders of the Church arise and weep and cry between the porch and the altar for the people? Vance Havner said, "Where is the prophet among the priests who will call the church to repentance?" Are we so gripped with apathy and indifference to not make a difference?

Allow me to end with a story about Charles Finney when he was a young handsome preacher, laboring in upstate New York in 1824. Having no formal training for the ministry, he desired not to labor in large urban areas but rather took his message to new settlements where his pulpit was in school houses, barns, and groves. As he preached in a small village in Evan's Mills, he recorded the following:

> More or less convictions occurred under every sermon that I preached; but still no general conviction appeared upon the public mind. I was very much dissatisfied with this state of things; and at one of my evening services, after having preached there two or three Sabbaths and several evenings in the week, I told the people at the close of my sermon, that I had come there to secure the salvation of their souls. That my preaching, I knew, was highly complimented by them; but that after all, I did not come there to please them but to bring them to repentance. That it mattered not to me how well they were pleased with my preaching, if after all they rejected my Master.

Finney cared little what man thought of him; he cared greatly what God thought of him. If we are honest with ourselves we too would rather please God than man; why not act like it? What is keeping us from realigning ourselves and our ministries to seek eternal things over our things? We had better have an answer for we will answer one day to Him who has eyes like fire.

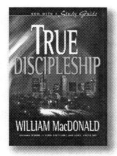
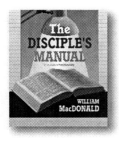